THE MIND AND ART OF CHAUCER

THE MIND AND ART OF

Chaucer

by J. S. P. TATLOCK

GORDIAN PRESS, INC.
NEW YORK
1966

Originally Published 1950
Reprinted 1966

Printed in U.S.A. by
EDWARDS BROTHERS INC.
Ann Arbor, Michigan

INTRODUCTION

I T WOULD be hard indeed to think of any important
problem of Chaucerian scholarship that has not received
the imprint of Dr. Tatlock's clear and vigorous mind, his
vast learning, and above all his genius for seizing the essentials. The bibliography printed at the end of this volume
bears witness to the scope of his contributions in this field.
They range from close studies of questions of chronology,
sources, manuscript tradition, etc., to brilliant reinterpreta-
tions of Chaucer's masterpieces and a translation of his complete works, *The Modern Reader's Chaucer,* to say nothing of
scores of short notes and reviews and, last but not least, the
Chaucer Concordance. Yet even more striking than Tatlock's
command of this field was his learning on the Middle Ages
in general—on their history, political institutions, social and
economic conditions, on philosophy and religion, on folklore and, needless to say, languages. Kindled by a vivid
imagination and sifted and integrated, this rich learning had
led to extraordinarily full and definite pictures of various
periods of the Middle Ages, especially the England of the
twelfth and of the fourteenth century and Dante's Italy. But
while he saw and made his readers see these periods as in
many respects sharply differentiated, the feature that struck
him as most important was found common to all: from
Boethius to Chaucer he saw the Middle Ages as preeminently
rationalistic, their greatest achievements the products of disciplined minds in pursuit of aims primarily ethical and in-

tellectual. On this trait he would lay stress again and again, in the classroom and in print; it may well be called the keystone of his view of the Middle Ages, and no doubt is the chief reason why he felt so entirely at home in the society of the great medievals and why their concepts were analysed and compared to ours not only with absolute open-mindedness but with a ready sympathy far from common, alas, among non-Catholic medievalists.

Another striking feature of Professor Tatlock's contributions to medieval scholarship is well illustrated in this book. I have already referred to the fulness and definiteness of his pictures of certain periods of the Middle Ages. This enabled him to form unusually definite ideas of the extent to which Dante, for instance, or Chaucer or Geoffrey of Monmouth were representative of their times as against the extent, delineated with equal sureness, to which, by the strength of their personality, as men and as artists, they had transcended their century. The very precise distinctions to which this led are one of the most characteristic features of Tatlock's writings, and of course have contributed greatly to our understanding of Chaucer and others.

It is in the realm of aesthetics, where vagueness is not always easy to avoid, that the precise distinctions and delineations in which Tatlock excelled are perhaps most helpful and stimulating. His reactions to art—plastic art as well as literature—were extremely keen. They have often found expression in phrases that cling to the memory, as when, commenting on the variety of "tone, pitch, key and mode" in the *Canterbury Tales*, he called the *Knight's Tale* "gallant and poetically decorative, but detached; the *Miller's, Reeve's* and *Sumner's* keen on the surface and light-heartedly animal; the *Shipman's* more refined and worldly, more disillusioned; the *Man of Law's* leisurely, imposing, and aloof, rhetorically rather than poetically decorative; . . . the *Pardoner's* simple yet full of deep insight, and matchless for uncanny mystery; . . . the *Squire's* romantic yet lifelike wall-painting; the

Franklin's an exquisite blend of reality and the ideal, of the marvelous and the homely; the *Second Nun's* entering with imaginative sympathy into an ideal largely bygone even to Chaucer." (*Mod. Phil.*, XXXIII, pp. 380-81).—No wonder that Dr. Tatlock, as I have often heard him say, never tired of giving his Chaucer course!

The present book is the last of Tatlock's writings. He began it in 1946 after completing an important work soon to come off the press, *The Legendary History of Britain,* to which he had devoted most of his time the previous twelve or fifteen years. On Chaucer he was to write briefly, giving the chief facts on his life and works with only here and there brief indication of the evidence on debatable points. But health failed; the last section, on the *Canterbury Tales,* was written under strain and covers only the first four of the Tales. That this is deeply to be regretted need hardly be said, and indeed is only too obvious from the passage just quoted. Yet I am not sure that the written chapters, dealing as they do with works less widely read, may not provide the non-specialist lover of Chaucer with what he needs most: from an authoritative pen and in characteristically condensed form (Dr. Tatlock, it has been said, never wasted his reader's time), the main facts of the poet's life and its background, political, social, intellectual, and artistic; the chief facts also on the early works and on their sources, the relations indicated with Tatlock's well-known grasp of the larger problems of literary history. Seen as he makes us see them, such poems as the *House of Fame* and the *Parliament of Fowls* become fascinating in themselves, to say nothing of our clearer understanding of their importance as landmarks in the development of the poet's genius. It is the emphasis laid throughout the book on Chaucer's personality and on his art that has suggested the title *The Mind and Art of Chaucer.*

But the book is not only for the general reader. If in the last fifteen years of his life, Tatlock wrote few articles on Chaucer, his interest in Chaucerian scholarship never slackened, and, as might be expected, some of his views were altered, either because the same facts, on reconsideration, were given a different interpretation, or more often because of the fresh evidence which other scholars were supplying. Here then we have the last considered opinion of this eminent Chaucerian on such matters as the date of the *Troilus,* where he courageously maintains the view propounded in earlier writings; on the allegorical interpretation of the *Parliament of Fowls* and on the likelihood that Chaucer read the *Decameron,* on each of which his former position is here abandoned. I may add that, while Dr. Tatlock had of course not given every one of the written chapters the final touch and we were forced to do some editing, neither the little changes which Professor Sanford B. Meech and I have made in a few sections nor his slight and skilful rephrasing of a sentence here and there have in the least affected the meaning.

In closing I would like to quote from a letter of Professor Walter Morris Hart, whose distinguished work on Chaucer and life-long friendship with Dr. Tatlock lend especial interest to his comments on this book. "With Tatlock," Dr. Hart writes, "the style, to an unusual degree, was the man. Reading these pages I had constantly the sense of his presence, of his own special personality, his gaily defiant manner (as when, sometimes to his friends' dismay, he drove his car). In the very informality and casualness of the style there is something warmly human, to use a phrase he liked. Lightly carrying a vast amount of learning he seemed always to be saying what he newly and freshly felt rather than something 'recollected in tranquillity' and coldly formulated. The result, to me, is a sense of new closeness to Chaucer, a new understanding of so much that was admirable and that I had overlooked."

"A sense of new closeness to Chaucer"—it is my wish and my hope that the reader will share this experience with Dr. Hart.

GERMAINE DEMPSTER.

Chicago, January, 1950.

CONTENTS

Forget six counties overhung with smoke,
Forget the snorting steam and piston stroke,
Forget the spreading of the hideous town;
Think rather of the pack-horse on the down,
And dream of London, small, and white, and clean,
The clear Thames bordered by its gardens green;
Think, that below bridge the green lapping waves
Smite some few keels that bear Levantine staves,
Cut from the yew wood on the burnt-up hill,
And pointed jars that Greek hands toiled to fill,
And treasured scenty spice from some far sea,
Florence gold cloth, and Ypres napery,
And cloth of Bruges, and hogsheads of Guienne;
While nigh the thronged wharf Geoffrey Chaucer's pen
Moves over bills of lading.

WILLIAM MORRIS: *The Earthly Paradise*

CHAPTER ONE

LONDON, CHAUCER, AND HIS ENGLISH GENERATION

WILLIAM MORRIS' familiar lines give the best sketch of his master Chaucer at his principal calling, and against its visible background though a trifle idealized; and the meaning of all of it—Chaucer was a Londoner through and through. London, though much smaller than Paris, was one of the richest and greatest cities of Europe. What had made it so was commerce, importing wine and spicery and cloth, among the chief things, and exporting the wool that made the cloth; fish came from Iceland, wine from Greece, and furs from the Baltic coasts—the three corners of Europe. Citizens of London possessed special privileges in other parts of Engand; it claimed and made good a special voice in the choice of a new king, the sovereign was forced to allow it special rights and independence; ceremonially to this day the king asks permission to enter London City. The individual town was the starting-point of English individuality and English freedom; small towns were sticklers for their rights and privileges, and made commercial treaties with each other like England and France. London above all was the starting-point of English democracy, or rather oligarchy at first.

The size, wealth, and situation of London near the continent of Europe were making it, together with the adjacent Westminster, what we should call the capital of the country.

Since the reign of Edward I, parliament had regularly met in Westminster; more and more this was the seat of government; of many residences of the sovereign, several were thereabouts. No longer, as earlier partly owing to difficulties in transporting food, was the court like other great households frequently on the move from one estate to another. London was usually the scene of its splendor and luxury, which in the fourteenth century, as earlier, far surpassed anything that we see today. Our privileged classes are fearful of exciting the ill-will of others by display; in Chaucer's day there was little social jealousy. To see the dazzling magnificence of their betters was one thing which reconciled the rabble to hardship; social distinctions were taken as the order of nature. Good taste did not forbid splurge. The chief survival of medieval splendor today is in the church, but that is mostly within doors. As lately as a half-century ago, the army produced brilliant pageantry; now that the military have become grimly practical, what most recalls medieval everyday show is a solemn high mass. But splendor and ritual in Chaucer's day produced no awe, were taken for granted, were every-day matter-of-course. The pageantry, the visible variety of classes, the picturesqueness and splendor of medieval society are reflected in its literature. At its best, this has firm grasp of the essentials and variety of human motive and personality, but it is less their analysis and origins which concern it than human appearances and behavior.

The walled city of London extended east and west along the river Thames less than a mile and a half, and northwards hardly a half mile. The population in 1380 was upward of 20,000 above the age of fifteen. The city was grey and brown with stone and weathered wood and thatch, or reddish with tile; dirty and untidy, in spite of well-meaning laws, impractical, ignoring human nature as medieval laws were so apt to do (though we might remember a recent law in an eastern American state requiring the removal of all weeds from everyone's real-estate). Refuse went out at the windows, and slaughtering was done in the streets, as in modern Athens. But hogs, unclaimed dogs, and scavenger birds besides contributing their own helped to keep the refuse down; streams ran through the town into the Thames, and the abundant rain washed things off such pavement as there was and away through gutters. Dung, blood, bits of food littered the street, but not burnt matches, cigarette-ends, newspapers. Indeed one might walk London from end to end and never see a written word; before printing and with an illiterate populace, signs were not written but symbolical, as the custom survives in our striped posts for a barber and three balls for a pawnbroker.

The principal streets were fairly wide, though often encroached on, minor streets narrow and irregular, the four or five-story houses with upper floors projecting in order to gain space, but cutting off light. Also to economize space in the protected city, on London Bridge (the only bridge) were houses and shops, and there were houses on top of the city wall, not so well protected one might think, but this well exhibits the freedom of England from invasion and major warfare. The mansion built over Aldgate was allowed (seemingly rent-free) by the mayor of the city to Chaucer in 1374, with the proviso that it might be resumed if needed in time of war. Such domiciles are thought to have been sought after, being quiet, airy, and bright, like tall apartment-houses today. To the west, where the prevailing westerly winds kept the air fresh, toward the governmental concentration of Westminster outside the walled city were great houses with spacious gardens. But suburbs in general were shabby places for living, the abode of such as Chaucer's alchemists and other shady persons. In this city Chaucer was born, here he died, and here, except for some years after 1385 and when duty took him away, were his home and the sights he saw every day.

Chaucer's people came from Ipswich, a chief river-seaport in Suffolk, which handled much the same foreign merchan-

dise as London, since the qualifications of a great seaport
were less exacting than today. Robert, his grandfather, was
enterprising enough to establish himself in London. His
father, John Chaucer, was fairly well-to-do, had associations
with the king, and like Robert and other relatives held offices in the king's customs. While Geoffrey's personality and
abilities raised his social standing higher, he was not a self-
made man, and started life with advantages. He came of
better middle-class folk, with the opportunities for familiarity with the upper class all the way to the top, which, in a
relatively small community such as medieval England, may
befall men of sense and charm.

We know from his vague but legally-recorded words that
he was born in the 1340's, and a date about 1343 well fits
all known facts. We know little about his formal education.
Indeed till two generations ago, amazingly little had been
reliably and exactly ascertained about medieval elementary
schools. But there is good reason to suppose that in his boy-
hood he attended one of the three old grammar-schools main-
tained by St. Paul's cathedral and the churches of St. Mary-
le-Bow and St. Martin-le-Grand; one of these rather than a
little choir-school, rather perhaps also than a gild-school. The
word grammar, "grammatica," in the Middle Ages meant the
Latin language, spoken and written, and Latin literature.
Latin was the language for the whole of the curriculum,
construed then into French, not English. Both Latin and
French were necessary for all educated men, and official documents such as Chaucer later was concerned with were in one
or the other. When the recent studies on Chaucer's education
and reading by the ever-regretted Karl Young see the light,
we shall know more about the books read, but they would
doubtless include the *Liber Catonianus* or Distichs of Cato,
and the *Primarium* or Primer, containing parts of the liturgy
specially used by the laity.

A rather good case has also been made out for his having
been much later a student at the law school in the Inner

Temple. This is based on a curious report, which has been thoroughly scrutinized, of a notice seen in the sixteenth century in the Inner Temple records that "Geffrye Chaucer was fined two shillinges for beatinge a Franciscane Fryer in fletestreate." Here he would have had a chance for more than such ebullitions—to learn not only the law but other studies and accomplishments. But for these latter, and especially for his familiarity with French and its literature, we need think of no more than his early life at home and at school and his years in royal households. Henry IV, at the end of Chaucer's life, was the first sovereign whose usual language was not French, and the English court was full of French culture. But since the intellectual life was expressed in Latin, and medieval culture was based upon classical literature, so cultivated an intellectual as Chaucer no doubt constantly heard and even spoke it. Almost all the earlier writers whom he names, especially those he took seriously, and a large majority of those he uses without naming, wrote in Latin, classical or medieval. In his day, energetic minds were not afraid of foreign languages, even so difficult as Latin; Chaucer continued to read its literature out of his own free energy, although not scorning the help of French and Italian translations.

The first contemporary word of Geoffrey Chaucer himself is at the age of fourteen or so, early in 1357, as then in the household of the wife of Prince Lionel, second son of Edward III, and also there as late as 1358, traveling with the household about the country as far north as Yorkshire. Less money was spent on him than on others, and we may infer that he was young and unimportant, a page we might say. His duties, we may suppose, would be such as taking care of clothes and arms, running errands, carrying messages, bearing trains, holding torches, serving at meals, such humble services as would be dignified by the rank of those for whom they were done. One of Queen Victoria's maids of honor, daughter of a peer, is reported to have said she considered it an honor to hand the queen her stockings. (With the change in the times, Queen-mother Mary was the earliest sovereign to employ a hireling maid). Seemingly in October of 1360, as we learn from the Exchequer Accounts, Chaucer carried letters to England from Calais during peace negotiations there, and was called clerk of the king attached to the person of Prince Lionel.

After some years of which little is known (his time at the Inner Temple might come here), from 1367 on for years, he had a similar position in the household of the king. In documents he is mentioned in the usual phrase, as "dilectus vallettus noster." "Vallettus," literally merely "young man," even of noble birth, commonly rendered "yeoman," indicates some modest rank in the king's household not to be exactly defined, with duties still less definable. Since in 1367 he received a royal pension for life (which was normal), presumably he was valued through already long service to the king. In 1368, 1372-1377, he is labeled "squire" ("scutifer, armiger Regis"), seemingly higher than "vallettus," with duties probably miscellaneous and social. Such persons in Chaucer's day might be, but seemingly were not usually, of distinguished families. As has been shown, they had sometimes held like position in the household of one of the king's children, or their fathers had been connected with the court, both of which conditions are true of Chaucer. In fact the language used in referring to Chaucer, and grants made to him are not exceptional, but common with people of his station. The household was very large, all told numbering in his day nearly 400 (besides the queen's own huge household), and receiving good pay and also allowances and perquisites. It had its own law-court and was well regulated and disciplined (save that people often had to wait for money due them). The great hall was under "two knights marshal of the hall," who doubtless flashed into Chaucer's memory when he described the imposing Host of the Tabard Inn as seemly "to han been a marchal in an halle." Life was brilliant, with the medieval taste for shows, bright colors, ornament, garb varied for various ranks and offices, with flashing jewels on both men and women, in which both were fain to invest their money because of lack of banks, insurance, and other convenient forms of investment. Life was prodigal, luxurious and comfortable so far as comfort depends on service and ease, which in such a huge household even a minor member, if attractive, could in a measure enjoy; and it was entertaining, for the household included minstrels and falconers.

All that is certainly known of Chaucer's life between his service to Prince Lionel's wife and to the king is that he was made prisoner in France during a campaign of the Hundred Years War and was ransomed in March of 1360, along with the other young servitors of the royal family, the king's contribution for him being rather handsome compared with that for others. Ransoms were lucrative to the higher fighting classes; the practice contributed no doubt to the comparatively easy-going and humane character of later medieval warfare. Well-to-do prisoners were geese which laid golden eggs. Of course, since Chaucer knew French well long before this, the interlude as prisoner was unimportant in his life. That he was in the army as young as sixteen is nothing notable: At the battle of Poitiers, in 1356, King John of France had fighting with him his four sons, the two youngest being fifteen and fourteen. It is probable that it was soon after Chaucer's return to England that he entered the king's household. Again in 1369, he was in France on military service.

Chaucer's wife, married perhaps in 1366, was Philippa Roet, daughter of a Sir Payne Roet and lady-in-waiting to and doubtless namesake of the queen, a natural match for a king's squire. She apparently died in 1387. About the felicity of the marriage there are only surmises. Two sons were born; Thomas, a man of mark in the next century, and "Lyte Lowys my sone," who was doing well in arithmetic and eager to learn about the astrolabe at the age of ten, as the poet tells in the charming preface to his elementary treatise of 1391 on that instrument. One can hardly miss the tenderness in "for Latyn ne canst thou yit, but small, my litel sone." Other children have been guessed at, on the basis of some evidence.

From these domestic stations with royalty, Chaucer proceeded into the civil service. He was one of a goodly fellowship of wise literary men who have preferred this modest but secure calling which allowed trustworthy leisure for the writing they were anxious to do. He belongs in that group with Isaac Newton, Lamb, James and John Stuart Mill, and Matthew Arnold, and with Hawthorne and Howells who both did the same, but, with American changefulness, only for a time. From wearing routine and wearing problems, he had a snug spot where he could retire with his imagination. His early life as a man in the world was still contingent on the royal family. Aside from depending on the sovereign as a fount of office, honor, and income for many years, Chaucer and his wife may be called protégés of John of Gaunt, Edward's third and most forceful son. Not only did they receive annuities and gifts from him, they were in relation with all three of his wives. Chaucer's early poem, the *Book of the Duchess,* is a memorial elegy in honor of the first wife Blanche. Philippa Chaucer was in the service of the second, and the prince's third wife (previously mistress) was Philippa's own sister. There is a sixteenth-century statement that Chaucer's poem called *A B C* was written for the devotions of Duchess Blanche, and a statement of the fifteenth century that the *Complaint of Mars* was written at the command of John himself. But there is no proof that Chaucer's relation to John was in any way essential to a man whose whole official career was so unexceptional. While, through his powerful friends, Chaucer at times may have been affected by political ups and downs, there is no indication that he took part in party strife; his interests were elsewhere, he may have been too discreet, who shall say not too Laodicean? He stood by the king, rather than zealously by any mere faction. For one more significant matter, in all the records of Chaucer's life there is not a syllable to indicate that he was a literary man. There was little possibility then of an author obtaining revenue from the sale of his works. But those of Chaucer undoubtedly enhanced his notability and attractiveness, and won him handsome gifts from the great and the wealthy. Complimentary tributes in his works, presents of copies and reading them aloud (one of the great methods whereby Chaucer's poetry gained its vogue) would bring money rewards far beyond any expenses thus incurred by the poet. It was Chaucer the poet, undoubtedly, that promoted among the powerful the worldly standing of Chaucer the man.

Most of the national administrative system in England had developed out of the king's household, as much of its nomenclature shows: e.g., "Wardrobe," far from its original sense, came to mean financial and secretarial office, though financial originally only for buying clothes. In particular cases, it is often hard to know the implication and sense of a position or title. Since the personnel was selected by the king himself and men close to him, he had every chance to notice young men of unusual promise and capacity, and to put them into wider service. Many prominent men got their start in lowly ranks of the royal household. There, no doubt, Chaucer made the impression to which he ultimately owed most of his later offices.

This would assuredly be true of his diplomatic missions to Flanders, France, and Italy, of which he had nearly a dozen between 1368 and 1387. Such missions were frequent before permanent embassies were as now the general rule, all obviously calling for the personal traits which make a man trusted. The matters treated of in Chaucer's missions were often important, though mostly secret and now unknown. One in 1381 was so intimate as to deal with marriage negotiations, which came to nothing, between Richard II and the daughter of the French king; some had to do with the French war and peace negotiations, others with commercial matters. While he never seems to have been head of an important legation, he was often the second or third member of a very small one, and repeatedly received the letters patent of protection during absence which were issued to important legates. Among his other functions, therefore, he was a diplomatist. For his own career the most important missions were to Italy: in 1372-1373 to Genoa and Florence, in 1378 to Milan, involving in all at least four or five months stay in the country. There is little reason to doubt that this was when he learned the Italian language, and above all came under the influence of the three towering Trecentisti, who forced him from the ascendancy of fashionable French poetry, promoted the action on him of classical poetry, and freed his own literary personality—Dante the medieval epitome, Petrarch with his look both back and forward, and Boccaccio with his own extraordinary free originality and versatility. With Chaucer then began that Italian pull and example for literary England which was to be the chief contemporary European guide till the seventeenth century.

Chaucer's most lasting occupation was in the King's customs. This regular levy on a national basis goes back to 1275, but, of course, had its beginnings much earlier, either as a requital for the king's protection of trade or merely as a due to the royal prerogative; it was paid on both exports and imports, solely for revenue, and in either money or kind. The king's right to a certain number of tuns of wine out of a shipload explains his grant to Chaucer in 1374 of a daily pitcher of wine in the port of London at the hands of the king's butler or his lieutenant, an inconvenient gift, later commuted to a money payment, and repeated in other forms. It is the importance of the trade in wine imported in tuns which is the origin of our "tonnage" of a ship, and hence ton as a measure of weight. To follow back human practice as to beverages, like so many practices, is not a bad stimulus to the inward eye to see our ancestors as they were. They had no coffee, tea, "soft drinks," distilled liquors; water was unattractive to them, and thought unwholesome, with good reason, though not because it "chilled the stomach." They did not know boiling and other processes against the crafty microbe. Of course, they had such blameless liquids as milk, soup, cider. They used beer and other plebeian drinks, but the better sort drank copiously of wine.

In 1374 about a year after Chaucer's return from his mission in Italy, he was appointed comptroller in the port of London of the custom and subsidy of wools, hides, and wool-fells, and perhaps then also of the petty customs on wines and other merchandises, the two chief branches of the customs. It looks as if this prospect accounts for his lease only four weeks earlier of the house above Aldgate, only a half-mile or so from the custom-house. The customs-appointments carried the proviso that he should write out the rolls with his own hand and not by a substitute. We do not have to believe that this proviso was always insisted on, but we might perhaps infer from it not only governmental caution but also that he wrote a good clerkly hand, and therefore that no copyist's errors in his literary work were due to his own illegible handwriting. The chief duty of the comptroller of customs was to keep an eye on the accounts of the collectors, for there was much evasion and dishonesty. In 1377, the comptrollership for wools, etc., with the same proviso, was renewed by the boy Richard II, and so in 1378 were Edward III's annuities to Chaucer and his wife, and in 1382 the appointment in the petty customs; he stood in with the new administration. Licence granted in February of 1385 to have a permanent deputy as comptroller, as temporarily several times before, may have been partly a recognition that Chaucer's value for many duties had made the proviso as to his writing his rolls "manu sua propria" a dead-letter. There is proof that he continued to hold office till November of 1386, but in the next month both his offices in the customs were given to others. Some have suggested that this was due to the faction of the earl of Gloucester, the king's uncle, trying to make a clean sweep of the young king's appointees, but the records show no other changes of office at the time. The reason, then, is beyond our knowledge.

But not beyond another probable conjecture, Chaucer's own desire to substitute for metropolitan life the life of something like a country gentleman. At all events, the years 1385-1386 mark a turning-point in his life, for it is almost certain that in 1385 he became a resident in Kent (on which more anon), probably in the town of Greenwich. Evidence for this location is in the *Envoy à Scogan,* where Chaucer's lament at being forgotten "in solytarie wildernesse" is marginally glossed in all three manuscripts "à Grenewych." This gains some countenance from a line in the Reeve's prologue in the *Canterbury Tales;* as the pilgrims ride along,

> Lo Grenewych, ther many a shrewe is inne,

which sounds like a mere chaffing allusion to his own residence. For a time he may have very often visited London, the distance by that great thoroughfare the Thames being only some five miles to the customhouse, and we are not sure that he left his Aldgate house till October of 1386, when it was leased to another tenant. It may be that his absence on leave for most of December of 1384 concerned his acquiring property and moving to Kent, and the deputy allowed from February of 1385 was perhaps due to his having moved about that time.

That he not only resided in Kent but owned land in the county is almost proved by one of the most significant events in his private life, his appointment by the king in October, 1385 (renewed in June, 1386), as one of the sixteen justices of the peace for Kent. This office ("custos pacis," "justiciarius ad pacem," "justice de peas," etc.), a peculiarity of the English legal system, was firmly established by 1360 or earlier, and had to do with keeping order, and many matters such as labor and wages, and including exportation of wool. Court was held four times a year. The office was one step in the transition from feudalism to the government of the country mainly by the gentry which continued to the nineteenth century. Some justices were, though not necessarily, trained in the law, and Chaucer's experience at the Inner Temple (if actual) would doubtless have made him the more eligible. The main thing is that men appointed must be men of position and standing, and Chaucer's appointment so soon after his moving to Kent is a clear tribute to his standing and personality.

A similar tribute a little later looks in the same direction. In August or September of 1386, Chaucer as a "suitable and discerning man girded with a sword," was chosen as Knight of the Shire (not in the chivalric sense) for Kent to sit in the Parliament of October in that year at Westminster. The commoners in parliament were otherwise prominent men, but especially the two shire Knights, who were highly paid— double what Citizens and Burgesses received. Though the Knights were often reëlected, Chaucer never was; we have no means of knowing why, unless for political reasons. This position, also, as a high-ranking member-at-large so soon after Chaucer had become a resident of the county would seem to show how his standing and personality impressed people; so also his being treated as one of King Richard's scapegoats, if so he was.

If politics had something to do with his lack and loss of known offices about 1387-1388, Richard II's assumption of his prerogative in May of 1389 may be why Chaucer's fortunes seem to have improved. One of his most responsible positions he held under royal appointment for two years, from July, 1389, to June, 1391, namely; the office of Clerk of the King's Works at Westminster, the Tower, and many royal manors and other places in southeastern England. His duties were to engage workmen and buy materials for building and repairs, the structure oftenest mentioned as undergoing restoration being St. George's chapel at Windsor (not the present chapel, which is later). While the workmen mentioned were manual laborers, he must have dealt with architects or have acquired some of their art himself. His many-sided duties included even the selling of branches and bark of trees provided for buildings, to say nothing of matters unconnected with the king's palaces and manors, such as erecting scaffoldings for tournaments at Smithfield in 1390, and directing some building for the wool custom-house. Finally in March of 1390 he was appointed on a commission of six to survey the dilapidated dikes and bridges on the Thames just below London, and compel owners of adjoining property to repair them. During these years he controlled rather large sums of money, recommended for appointment deputies and agents for himself, and obviously had varied and business-like responsibilities, in widely scattered places. Since at this time he either was or would wish to be concentrated on imagining and composing the *Canterbury Tales,* we can believe that he would relish a less restless occupation.

The opportunity soon came through Chaucer's latest known position, which took him once more into the country, but to a remoter and quieter part. In 1390-1391, and again in 1397-1398, he was appointed one of two deputy-keepers of the small royal forest of North Petherton in Somerset. "Forest," of course, originally merely land outside ("foris") of an enclosed park, was a technical term for a large area mostly of woodland but containing farms and even towns. The primary purpose of a royal forest was for the king's hunting, a favorite sport important also for supplying meat, and it was controlled under "forest-law," superimposed and encroaching on the common-law. Chaucer's duties would involve little which is now called forestry, but would be supervision of a considerable staff for control of hunting, poaching, dogs, stray cattle, pasturage, wood-cutting, and encroachments by residents. This forest was some hundred and forty miles from Greenwich, and the duties presumably required much time in Somerset, though seemingly he retained his legal residence in Kent. It was probably during these North Petherton years that he formed a valuable and valued relationship with Henry, Earl of Derby, to whom, after he became King Henry IV, Chaucer addressed his latest datable work, the light but loyal *Com-*

plaint to his Purse. Thus from the beginning of his life to the end, as a man in this world his life was contingent on the reigning sovereign and his family.

The variety of Chaucer's occupations described above prepares one for the large number of minor occasional functions during the middle and latter part of his life, remunerative wardships, commissions, suretyships, brought him doubtless by his versatility, perceptiveness and humanity. Much money passed through his hands, and the evidence suggests that he was financially comfortable most of his life. There is a little evidence that during the time when he was seemingly out of office he was in straits and more to the same effect during the years 1395-1398, though presumably he was then still forester at North Petherton, unless the renewal of this appointment in 1397-1398 was due to his need of it. In May 1398, he feared complaints and suits might hinder him in "quamplura ardua et urgencia negocia" of the king, who accordingly issued for him a writ of protection. What is more startling, later in that year he could not be found and was threatened with arrest and even outlawry for the claims of one Isabella Bukholt. Whether this was a personal debt or a matter of dispute connected with the clerkship we cannot tell. At any rate the sums involved were not very large, not too large to be borrowed from his friends by a man of his standing if in straits. Formal documents are not always to be taken literally, and in bygone centuries are sometimes hard to interpret. Perhaps the affairs were small enough for him to be careless about, and one can well believe that Geoffrey Chaucer might at times be careless as well as prodigal when absorbed in the *Canterbury Tales.* And in these years, the *Life-Records of Chaucer* offer abundant evidence that, in connection with annuities, the royal finances were negligent and dilatory, perhaps the reason why grants which seem to the modern so remarkably generous were so frequently announced. Chaucer's income, like others', was largely made up in kind (such as the pitchers and butts of wine), clothing perquisites, annuities, gifts of all kinds which compensated for low official pay; his total actual income at any time is utterly impossible to estimate in either modern or medieval sums. In the customhouse or elsewhere we should not assume that at some of its sources the strict modern might not raise his eyebrows. Tacit customary gratifications, anywhere between a fee and a bribe, may in one generation be approved, then winked at, then frowned on when public morality takes a spurt forward, as Francis Bacon painfully learned. Needless to say, there is no sign that Chaucer was ever frowned on.

After his years in Kent and in Somerset, Chaucer in 1399 settled in Westminster. On Christmas Eve he took a lease for fifty-three years from the monks of Westminster of "unum tenementum" in the garden of their chapel of Blessed Mary, where Henry VII's chapel stands now. Though the lease might be ended at his death, yet some years later Thomas Chaucer is found paying rent on this house, a corroboration of contemporary record that he was a son.

It is practically certain that Chaucer died in 1400; the last recorded payment of money to him is of 5 June in that year, and the date of death put on his altar-tomb was 25 October, 1400. It is not certain that this exact date is reliable, since the tomb appears to be of the sixteenth century; nor whether the body was not at some time moved. But it cannot be doubted that his burial in Westminster Abbey was due to his having been a tenant of its monks, as well as to the strong medieval sentiment for burial in a church. About two centuries later, Edmund Spenser was fittingly buried close by Chaucer, and afterwards the long succession of literary men which has brought the south transept the name "Poets' Corner," the most illustrious necropolis in history, and a highly decorative consequence of Chaucer's lease from the Westminster monks.

By a curious combination of circumstances, we know something of Chaucer's physique. When Browning's grave next to his was dug in the Abbey, Chaucer's bones were unearthed, and measurements of the chief long bones showed his height to have been about five foot six. The amusing words about his figure in middle age dramatically given in the prologue to the *Tale of Sir Thopas,*

> This were a popet in an arm t'enbrace,

show him to have been stoutish, which is backed up by sportive hints in other poems and by more or less authentic though somewhat crude portraits. The face in these, though pleasant and attractive, does not suggest a handsome person. His habit of disclaiming any experience or qualifications in love suggests a shrewd and tactful man averting the chaff which a poet, reading his love-poetry aloud, might well rouse by an unromantic face and figure.

Chaucer's prudence in seemingly keeping clear of politics, save as was required for retaining royal favor, doing his work in the world, otherwise merely observing it, surrendering to his imagination and to his feeling for individual people—all this is no more marked than his dateless disregard of the weighty changes which in his day were going on in human society. Now and then, he uses a metaphor or makes an allusion in which the informed mind and sharp eye can detect his awareness of what was happening; that is about all. Every age is one of "transition," but when the changes affect the fundamentals of life the word is really significant. If medieval systems and civilization reached their climax in the thirteenth century, in the fourteenth they showed the signs of breaking down which led society into the modern, though people were not aware of the universality and scope of the changes. I will not enlarge on the spread of education; nor on the change (miscalled the revival of learning) from an uncritical filial attitude toward Latin literature to the attitude of modern scholarship; nor on the rise of capitalism and the loss of social unity in the industrial class; nor on changes in the structure of society, social dislocations and accelerated social changes caused by the decay of the manorial system and by a series of dreadful pestilences and reduction of population which resulted in labor troubles and insurrection and socialistic and heretical tendencies; nor on the emphasis on nationality and intensifying of patriotism which soon made a purely dynastic and king's war, such as that called of the Hundred Years, become a thing of the past. Looking back we can see that more fundamental were social and religious changes. Feudalism had never worked very well, but in Chaucer's day it was breaking up in England in favor of democracy and a strong monarchy. Its accompaniment, the mounted knight, in spite of his survival in the Knight in Chaucer's *Prologue,* as a practical element in warfare was giving way before gunpowder, the long-bow, and the cross-bow. Disturbed above all were religion and the church. The domination of Pope Innocent III lay a century and a half in the past; through most of the fourteenth century till 1377, the prestige of the papacy in Avignon was marred through its domination by the French sovereign, and after that by the split of the Great Schism, with two popes, in Avignon and in Rome. The spiritual quickening brought by the friars in the thirteenth century had died down, and however sympathetic one may be with the medieval church, one has the feeling that its worldliness detracted from its moral dominance, and even from faith in religion. If the church had not greatly deteriorated, it is certain that people were more critical of it. The new spiritual and moral force now was half outside the church, in Wyclif and his preachers and translation of the Bible. Wyclif's anticlericalism commended him to many of the laity, notably for political reasons to Chaucer's friend John of Gaunt. Yet save as one can detect in spots in Chaucer sympathies harmonious with Wyclif's views—and he was no proclerical— there is not a syllable in his works to show his awareness of what was going on.

Characteristic medieval institutions were wearing thin as one might say in the fourteenth and fifteenth centuries, losing the momentum which buoyed men and their literature up and along, and there were no great new ideas to take their place. That is the reason for the poverty of literature in fifteenth-century England—not the Wars of the Roses for a few years, once propounded as its cause. And that is the reason for the vein of pessimism so startling in those centuries, to be felt in *Piers Plowman,* Gower, Wyclif, Lydgate, and the early Scottish poets. There was a paradox in the spirit of medieval man. Though philosophy as to the whole future of man sunned itself in the optimism of faith, its view of this present life, having no belief in the progress of earthly man onward and upward forever, was always pessimistic, and now an increase of outspoken religious scepticism turned eyes from God's future to man's present. When medieval ecstatic contemplation of God and perfection allowed the weary eye to sink to mundane things, no wonder it was shocked. Langland's discouragement about man left him no hope except in more religion and more morality, which was just another way of stating the grounds of his discouragement. The censorious gloom pervading the verses of Chaucer's moral and trustworthy friend John Gower, with less mystical faith than Langland, is an intensification of the usual medieval pessimism about this world. His favorite symbol is the image in Nebuchadnezzar's vision, early in the Book of Daniel, with head of gold, breast of silver, and declining down to feet of mingled iron and clay. This symbol was the basis of the chief medieval philosophy of history, wholly pessimistic as to mundane history, and Gower uses it in the seventh book of *Vox Clamantis* and the prologue of *Confessio Amantis.* We are living seemingly in the toes, of steel as he says and potter's earth.

Chaucer has none of this. He was as aware of the state of all classes of men as his contemporaries were, and at some time of his life he must have asked himself the question, What shall I write? He faced two dilemmas. One was that of language. It would have been easy, possibly better for his fashionable repute, to have chosen French; possible, though probably much less easy, to choose Latin. Very likely some of his lost poems were in these languages, though Chaucer's fluency in Latin may be doubted. The escape of the *Troilus* and the *Canterbury Tales* from a foreign language gives one a startled feeling, like Dante's known rejection of Latin for the *Divina Commedia*, the greatest escape of all escapes in literary history. The other dilemma was what part of reality he should face and embrace. Here his temperament, full of hope and good-will, turned him toward the cheerful side of that whole reality which is neither bad nor good. He not only shunned the faultfinding which thoughtful medievals were so prone to, he did not even write of the surface of life as he saw it; his photography used more penetrating rays. Though the life he knew best was that of a public servant, there is no public servant in the gallery of the Prologue to the *Canterbury Tales,* or elsewhere. His experience at court gives him a firm step in such tales as the Knight's, the Merchant's, and the Squire's. The London society under his eye all the time rarely appears; the setting of the Canon Yeoman's, however, is a disreputable suburb, and the Cook's fragment has a vivid glimpse of street-life, which suggests what the finished tale might have given us. So keen and analytic a man must have been aware of change as change, but his poetry was for him an escape from the hum-drum everyday. He is "modern" in the sense that he is timeless and deals with the human essence.

CHAPTER TWO

CHAUCER AND THE FRENCH TRADITION
The Roman de la Rose, The Book of the Duchess

THE YOUNG Chaucer, like most sociable young men, no doubt looked up to the dazzling society of his superiors in the royal household where he lived from the age of fourteen or so for the best part of twenty years. If as probably even then he had a penetrating and charitably satiric eye, this does not show in his early works. He would reach out toward their literary taste receptively, would share it more than we do, would see more value in the poetry they read. This fashionable poetry was all in French. Chaucer never grew beyond the influence of French literature; to the end of his life he cites and quotes it, but in his early years it was the sole contemporary influence on him.

In France as in England the literature taken most seriously was in Latin. In France, still more in Italy (as not in England), the vernacular had long been regarded as a mere concession to the uneducated, as the easy-going flow of spoken Latin which carried on the affairs of daily life. French was called "la langue romane" ("illa lingua romana"), the speech of the city of Rome which Roman soldiers and settlers had carried all over south and west Europe, while with them went also Latin, the written language of their literature, law, learning, and religion. It is true that by Chaucer's day French was well established as an independent entity, had been more and more so for three centuries, but only to the extent that in France it was now the main language, not of the intellectual nucleus, but of the polite as well as the crude, and this last was almost as true of French in England as in France. The meaning of the words "roman," "romance," in both French and English was the French language or a poem written in it, usually with no suggestion of what we call "romantic."

Throughout Chaucer's life the French work which most influenced him was the *Roman de la Rose,* than which there is no more glaring case of "this too shall pass away." Among the most dominant of poems throughout western Europe, it is now scarcely read except by literary historians. Its diffuseness and its rambling, its lack of steady aim and temper, its clashing of charming unreality with rude, sometimes unfair, realism (much of it bygone) may weary and repel the disinterested modern. But both the latter aspects were so fresh and brilliant to the thirteenth century that the very lack of harmony was stimulating. The expert Chaucerian is constantly startled when reading either the *Roman* or Chaucer to find how many passages even in his late poems are filched from the *Roman,* though it lacks his raciest and most human manner.

The clashing in the *Roman* was mainly due to double authorship. Not far from 1230, young Guillaume de Lorris conceived this Art of Love and wrote over 4,000 lines of love-allegory. L'Amant, who carries the story, dreams that in the month of May he is admitted by a beautiful girl named Idleness into an exquisite garden full of happy attractive people in their teens, dressed in the latest fashion. The portress' name reveals all; this love though intense is not deep, but for idle people, or at least idle moments; it produces no *Vita Nuova* or *Paradiso.* L'Amant sees a rose, which he longs to pick. His experiences before he attains his wish form the scheme of the entire long poem, the allegory of which is simple and plain. He is encouraged by what makes a girl receptive, Fair-Welcome, Pity, Generosity, and the like, opposed by what makes her hold off, Reserve (called "Dan-ger"), Fear, Scandal ("Evil-Tongue") and others. All is ci-vilized, normal, full of the beauty of privileged youth, at bottom conventional. Young Guillaume died at the point where L'Amant is uttering one of his prolonged lover's la-ments, because Fair-Welcome has been imprisoned to prevent mischief. The love is looking toward physical consummation, not specially marriage, but the possibility of this is recog-nized, without interest. The allegory is of the first experiences of sex-attraction, not of mature love. The superficial refine-ment and attractiveness in the embodying of this are clear. There is nothing innocent, the ideal is good taste. Any per-ceptive reader sees that the poet's consciousness is full of sensuality and even sensual experience, and that the refine-ment is meant to please a particular kind of audience, who find charm in sensual willingness without perhaps experience. These are patrician women and those sharing their taste, who liked to be shown love as an elegant amusement and to be allowed to ignore its violence and danger if they wished to do so. Such women set the mode for fashionable poetry. But Guillaume is not a boy; though young, he is mature. Certain literary elements here anyone who knows Chaucer will recognize as having passed on into his earlier poetry, and mainly from the *Roman,* though found in countless other things he had read—the springtime, the exquisite gar-den, the allegory and personification, the irresponsible setting in a dream.

Forty years later Jean Clopinel (de Meun) took up the parable. The inevitable course of the narrative proceeds, but with less action than before, little as that is, and with far more dialogue. Much of this is discoursing, especially by Reason, who gives excellent advice in favor of having babies and accepting actualities in the man-woman relation; dis-course also by Nature and others about the physical universe, philosophical and worldly matters, social inconsistencies, and other things unconnected with love. Jean's poetry has a good

deal of the irrelevant encyclopedic learning which intelligent
medievals relished, and which is an important element in
Dante's *Divina Commedia*. The irrelevance of much of this
did not strike readers unfavorably. Some of the opinions may
be passed off as those of the abstractions who utter them, and
not expressly Jean's, but there is no doubt that he is matter-
of-fact, contemptuous toward women and to the sentimental
Amant, despising lovers' laments and tears as unmanly, re-
bounding into defiance of sentimentality to the point of gross
but imaginative obscenity, despising prudery. If Guillaume
consulted feminine taste, Jean emphatically wrote for males.
He was highly intelligent and well-read, and, while not flout-
ing Christianity, conveying purely worldly wisdom worthy of
Horace and an immense selection from the learning and good
sense of the past. Both parts highly appealed to Chaucer,
but he outgrew Guillaume, though never Jean. The latter
might well appeal to the same readers who valued Guillaume.
There is no reason to believe Jean too wrote for any but
upper-class worldly people, who were not scholars but relished the wisdom which scholarship could give them; the
same class as Guillaume wrote for, but the more mature and
intelligent members of it. There is no ground for stating that
Guillaume wrote for the upper class and Jean for the
bourgeois.

The *Roman,* and later French imitations of it, were so
fundamental for Chaucer's early poetry that this is reason
enough for a full description of it. But more than this, we
have his own word for it in the prologue of his *Legend of
Good Women* that he translated the *Roman,* a translation
mentioned by his disciple John Lydgate, and also by his ad-
miring French friend, Eustache Deschamps. Further, we have
extant in two texts a fragmentary translation (7,696 lines)
from about his time. The first fragment, some 1,705 lines,
well done, though hardly distinguished, may be Chaucer's;
the second cannot possibly be, for it frequently uses a Northern dialect for convenience in riming, and also is very diffuse

in style, and otherwise inferior. The two are continuous, and translate less than the first quarter of the French; then after a gap of nearly the same extent, comes the third fragment which breaks off a little more than half through the French, and may be Chaucer's, though this seems less likely than in the case of the first. But whether Chaucer translated only small portions of the *Roman* or much or the whole of it— and neither his own reference nor those of Lydgate and Deschamps make this clear—it looks as though he had valued his translation but little, neglecting to protect it by having copies multiplied. The usual opinion that it was an early work is the probable one; as with a half dozen of his works, he may have lost interest and have been drawn away by something with more appeal to him. It is quite possible that the first extant fragment is all he ever wrote. The facts that the God of Love in the later *Legend of Good Women* reproaches him for writing of faithless Criseyde, and for translating

> the Romaunce of the Rose,
> That is an heresye ayeins my lawe,

but that none of the extant version has any of Jean's extensive slurs against love and women cannot be thought conclusive. We have here, not legal pleading, but an imaginative introducing of an amends for having associated himself with any part of a poem strongly discouraging to love. In a light vein, Chaucer might be merely giving Love a stronger case against him than the *Troilus* alone would have been.

In France the poetry of the fourteenth century was inferior to that in England; it had no Chaucer. The most characteristic and perhaps the most fertile manner followed the example of Guillaume in the *Roman de la Rose,* and was used by and for the fashionable. It shows Chaucer's gregariousness and agreeable modesty that till he was in his thirties this verse along with the *Roman* was the chief influence on

him. The poets were attached to courts, and in spite of the
faintness of their charm, their lack of power and originality,
they appealed to others who wished to please courts. The
three to mention are Guillaume de Machault, Jean Froissart
(more valued now for his enlivening chronicles), and Eustache Deschamps, the latest.

The first two of these men were the starting-points of
Chaucer's earliest datable poem, the *Book of the Duchess.*
Its opening lines,

> I have gret wonder, be this lyght,
> How that I lyve, for day ne nyght
> I may nat slepe wel nygh noght,

come straight from the opening of Froissart's *Paradys d'Amour*

> Je sui de moi en grant merveille
> Comment je vifs quant tant je veille.

Of this poem there are other reminiscences, as well as reminiscences of many more poems of this school. The chief source
is Machault's *Le Jugement dou Roy de Behaigne,* a highly
melodious poem by the most original of these three French-
men, lengthy, without special insight, turning the surface of
things over and over, as contemporaries liked, but highly
admired for generations. On a May morning in a gentle woodland, a lover overhears a sympathetic discussion between a
lady whose lover has died and a mild knight whose lady,
some fourteen years of age, evidently too young for passion,
counsels him to go to Love for help, not to her, but who has
presently accepted him, and then cast him off in favor of
another. Which of the two debaters is worse off? Wishing
to help the decision, the lover approaches, is revealed by the
lady's little barking dog, and suggests as umpire the king of
Bohemia, Machault's masculine but romantic patron. Though
it is not in dream-form Chaucer's inspiration from this is
plain. It is not to be supposed that he was making a deliberate patchwork out of all or any of these poems, still less that
as he wrote they all lay open before him, though he may have

reopened them to recall a tantalizing phrase. Their conceptions, situations, and even their words had flowed into his singularly tenacious memory and were there at will to help body forth what his quickening imagination was reaching out to conceive.

Chaucer is preeminently a narrator, and therefore here his poem does not surrender to the repetitious lyric style or mood for as long as Machault's does and therefore is not so lengthy; just so the *Troilus* restrains lyric expression far more than its original in Boccaccio does. The poet is sleepless and sad, for hopeless love we are meant to infer, and his servant gives him a book in French, "a romaunce,"

> To rede, and drive the night away,

better than chess or tables. This imaginary French book takes from Ovid's *Metamorphoses* one of his most moving stories, that of the mutual wedded love of Ceyx and Alcyone, who were changed into the halcyon birds, at whose nesting the winds are quiet for seven days. Chaucer's version is less moving than Ovid's, one-sided, concerns only the wife's grief, and is less fitting to the rest of his poem, which is only of a bereaved husband's love; but he imparts to this narrative a gentle drowsy feeling and a simple-mindedness which fit a certain unreality in the rest, and assuredly prepare for the dream. The length and partial irrelevance of this introductory passage appear in other of Chaucer's early poems, and would have hardly struck the medievals, who valued reminiscences of the classics (which they admired even if they did not read them) and lacked a sense of unity, proportion, and structure. The Greeks showed this sense in both poetry and architecture; the English, while they had such great churches as York or Lichfield, were prone to excrescences in later styles and inorganic in function, and in poetry were apt to drift unless they used, as Dante and Gower did, the regimentation of the scholastics. Only late in his life, did Chaucer cultivate a subtler unity.

In his dream the poet mounts his horse and joins a lifelike scene of hunting, but the hunt finds no game. Then the
dreamer is afoot, in a forest full of bucks—inconsequent, like
a dream—but Chaucer had insight into dreams. A puppy appears and "fawns him," and leads him on through the grand
but open medieval forest, the puppy as lifelike as the countless other mild animals,

> many squirelles, that sete
> Ful high upon the trees and ete,
> And in hir maner made festes,

and prepares us for Chaucer's liking for other beasts in later
poems. The dreamer becomes aware of a handsome man in
black, and overhears his "complaint" that death has taken his
lady sweet (It has eleven lines—that overheard in Froissart's
Fonteinne Amoureuse has eight hundred). Overhearing is a
commonplace in such poems, like soliloquy in later drama,
being a dramatic way of conveying things to a reader. There
is but little eavesdropping here compared with all that in
Machault and Froissart, for which their editors seem need-
lessly apologetic. As we shall see later with Chaucer, our
ancestors had more robust momentum than critics of a generation ago had, and did not subject literary artifice to rules
of human intercourse. At any rate the dreamer discloses himself, not out of any sense of honor but from humaneness, to
the lover who is on the point of fainting. The rest of the
poem is dialogue—the dreamer urges him to tell of his sorrows, saying

> Paraunter hyt may ese youre herte,
> That semeth ful sek under your syde;

and thoroughly he does it, describes his lady, body and soul.
Besides statements by Chaucer and others to the same effect,
we know from the poem itself that this lady "is," or symbo-
lizes, John of Gaunt's first wife, Blanche of Lancaster,

> And goode faire White she het,

and the lover equally "is" John himself, for at the end he goes homeward to

> A long castel with walles white,
> . . . . on a ryche hil,

these lines pointing unmistakably to his titles as duke of Lancaster and earl of Richmond. The identifications give us the date of the poem as about 1370, for Blanche died late in 1369 (when John was almost thirty), and he married Constance of Castile in 1371. While the descriptions and narrative have many small lifelike touches of Chaucer at his best, of activity and vivacity, both lack his later pervasive distinction of style, and the two personages are less portraits than patrician ideals conventional in the kind of poem he was writing. This kind of poem was very essential in the growth of civilization, for it heightened the valuing of gentleness and ideality among the worldly which the very rough Middle Ages needed, and this has prepared and so far secured for us moderns a valuing of something beyond brutal power, which we need just as much. Gentleness and ideality, however, were not characteristic of medieval men and women; all the more, then, they liked to fancy one another to possess these traits. Yet Chaucer, while pleasing conventional readers by the lady's refined and exacting conduct, rejects for her the imaginary extremities of sending her lover as a test of devotion to Wallachia or Tartary or to

> Goo hoodles to the Drye Se
> And come hom by the Carrenar.

No one knows much about the actual Blanche, who may have had all the sweet, gentle pride of this lady or may not; but John's enemies might not have recognized the active, brave, dignified reality in this lover's self-distrust and timidity. In pictures of love such traits were esteemed by fashionable women, to whom John was far from indifferent. A symbolic portrait of him as an admired poetic type very unlike himself would be as readily acceptable to him and others as a portrait of Louis XIV under the figure of the god Mars to that monarch.

Indifference to human reality is most marked of all in the dreamer (who is in no sense Chaucer himself). Informed by the overheard soliloquy that the lover's grief is due to his lady's death, to say nothing of his garments of mourning and the loving reminiscence all through his prolonged monologue, at the end the dreamer is astounded to learn that she is dead. Perhaps such forgetfulness is dreamlike; indeed before telling his own whole story the lover seems to betray some impatience toward this woolgatherer and demands his attention. Further, the dreamer's bewildered apathy Chaucer might explain, though a scientific psychologist would not, by prolonged emotional brooding and sleeplessness. But no explanation of the dreamer's state of mind, without more warning than there is, will persuade most moderns, still less a medieval if he thought about it, to accept the contradiction without question. It is entirely unlike Chaucer's later way. He was given to subtleties inconspicuously inserted in a broad and simple outline of personality, like a painting with bold clear design, which on scrutiny proves to be filled with faint detail which rewards the seeing eye without contradicting the whole. He showed his expertness in this in several of the *Canterbury Tales,* but here he makes a really inexplicable blur. Perhaps the most reasonable defence for something irrational even in a dream is merely literary. Though this poem is almost brisk compared with others of the kind, it is repetitious and dilatory; at the end the dreamer and the reader alike are the better for being brought back to the world of reality by being startled into it. The poem ends, as Chaucer likes to end, with a sharp line. But why he should so bluntly at the beginning tell us that the lady is dead, though at the end he is to ignore this, who can say?

The main thing in the poem is touching and simple feeling, conveyed in a combination of literary usage with actuality as Chaucer knew it. The honest feeling and regret for the departed and for vanished happiness put it in a distinguished

and very English order of poem, from the elegiac lyrics of
Old English down through the *Pearl,* Spenser, Milton, Shel-
ley, Arnold.

The medievals' expression of how they liked to think of
love adopts the literary idiom everybody readily accepted in
their day. In Chaucer it was inevitably narrative, and employed the settings then liked, most of them far older than
the poems described above, and most of them relished because very unlike real life; medieval poetry was an escape
from real life. Medievals lived in a very rough world, and
felt relief in wandering by imagination into the fragile and
delicate. The dream-setting was an acceptable way of passing
out of actual life into an irresponsible world where the fancy
was free to find anything whatever. This may be why till toward the end of his life, till the *Canterbury Tales,* again and
again, Chaucer the lover of the real world, when he wished
to start letting his fancy loose, instead of entering directly
into the irresponsible imaginative, returned to this route by
way of the dream, in which, unquestionably, he had remark-
able interest and insight. Equally of course the embodiment
was patrician and gentle and refined, though sometimes tacitly sensual, with every physical attraction and assumption. It
was normal human love, of course eventually physical,
stripped to its essence. It was no more illicit love than married love, as it clearly is in the *Book of the Duchess* and as it
was in the actual relation there symbolized. The expression
of it was intended for ladies and for men who here accepted
their lead; they found the ideality a temporary relief and
rest after the violent brutal medieval world. The allegory and
generalized figures satisfied that basic trait of the medievals,
a desire for general not particular truth and significance,
rather than merely the individual or striking. These gave
what seemed a fuller understanding of life than they were
ready to find in the portrayal of individual men and their
experiences. Allegory seemed a shorter cut to ultimate reality
than the far more difficult portrayal of warmly human persons who are none the less illuminating to our conception of

all humanity. The outdoor background is garden or improved woodland, without crag or thicket; purely beautiful and safe, as in Italian painting of later centuries; rough or grand scenery is only in Hell with Dante's *Inferno* and as late as *Paradise Lost,* for on this earth it meant discomfort from the difficulty of reaching it and danger from the wild animals and lawless men which it harbored. Taste changed in the eighteenth century not because of any romantic movement but because advance in civilization allowed the sensitive to surrender to spiritual exaltation without distraction by discomfort and danger. Likewise the time is May. Those in more genial climes do not know the depressing effect on some from the darkness of the north European winter, and from the perpetual wet, dampness, and chill, all of it far worse in the dwellings of the medievals. The monotony was heightened by the discomfort of travel and getting about, and the sameness and unattractiveness of the food, the lack of fresh meat, fish, vegetables, and fruit. No wonder the medievals resorted to spices and stimulating drinks; and then came the Church to make things worse with the rigorous fast of Lent. Of course all these privations were taken for granted by those who knew nothing better, but who can wonder at the honest joy when it was all over for a season? Spring poems and scenes are as sincerely felt as any literature the Middle Ages produced. Monotonous and unreal as the elements described make a good deal of medieval ideal literature seem to us pampered moderns, imaginative sympathy makes us charitable, might even make us accept it enthusiastically.

Troilus and Criseyde

THE MOST important thing which ever happened to Chaucer as a writer was his months in Italy in 1373. Had his years in the custom-house come before this they might have given him already some knowledge of the language of Italy, with which England had important commercial relations; but there is no reason to suppose that he had any linguistic qualification for his embassy except his familiarity with French and with Latin, of which Italian was merely the local colloquial form. He had already proved his possession of the other traits to fit him for negotiation. This new broadening experience not only contributed greatly to his personal development but led to his use of the three eminent Trecentisti, and above all freed him from the domination of the French poetry of his day, elegant and charming but limited.

Of these Trecentisti the one who took least hold on him was Petrarch, though he speaks of him with admiration. This man was first and foremost a scholar and student, with a new attitude to the ancient and indeed the modern world which Chaucer was not ready to adopt. One of the sonnets to Laura he translated in the *Troilus,* but never used the sonnet-form, and shows no knowledge of the other lyrics; any other influence of Petrarch's original writings is unimportant. There is not the least reason to believe that Chaucer ever met him in person. So far as Chaucer found his way out of subjection to medieval literary custom, the way was his own. For Dante, Chaucer had deep reverence, and knew the *Divina Commedia* intimately throughout. Dante is the only purely vernacular poet for whom he uses the exalted word "poete," others being merely "makers," and Dante is the only mainly vernacular writer (except Granson, as a special compliment) whom he names—five times citing or quoting him as he would a classical poet, not to mention many other reminiscences. These facts are eloquent as to the medieval feeling about literature, languages, and the ancients. In one of his lyrics, he adopts Dante's *terza rima*. In classing Dante with the ancient poets, for his high seriousness, wisdom, power, and beauty, Chaucer shows his unerring instinct.

The reasons why he never names Boccaccio, though he owes far more to him than to Dante or Petrarch, are that Boccaccio lacked their power and classic distinction, that he delivered himself like a man of this world, and that it was mostly and very extensively Boccaccio's Italian works which he used. But since the medievals liked to feel that what they were reading was actual and authoritative, they were prone to claim for tradition and even invention some respectable and early authority. Truth to the Middle Ages was in the past. Therefore Chaucer several times ascribes his matter to an imaginary source, just as many a modern writer does, less gravely. That which Chaucer several times alleges is one Lollius, who is totally unknown as a writer on the Troy-story; on the source of the name no probable suggestion has ever been made.[1] Lollius is not Boccaccio, but a mere means of bespeaking illusion for the reader, in what is mostly a combination of Boccaccio and Chaucer's own invention.

---

[1] Dr. Tatlock would doubtless have changed his mind on this point had he known of Professor Robert A. Pratt's recent finds about Horace, *Epistolae*, I, ii. It had previously been suggested that a scribal mistake of the most usual type in the first line of that *Epistola* might have caused the name Lollius to be taken as that of a writer on the Trojan War. That such was the origin of Chaucer's Lollius seems certain now from the form

The above-mentioned traits of Boccaccio made him more appealing and useful to Chaucer; so did his modesty and warm humanity, and his extraordinary originality in inventing fresh literary forms make him more congenial. Two of Chaucer's longest poems, the *Troilus* and the *Knight's Tale,* owe their matter and much of their actual wording to Boccacio. To Boccaccio he owes certain elements of style. His keen perception of the impressiveness of dramatic irony he owes mostly to Boccaccio and the often crude French fabliaux, and he gained from this a conception of plot more complex than the single-file of usual vernacular narratives. With Shakespeare and Thomas Hardy, Chaucer may be called the English writer who understood dramatic irony best. Further, from Boccaccio he learned the possibility of an elaborated narrative in long, leisurely stanzas. The stanza in seven ten-syllable lines is used throughout the *Troilus* and many others of his narratives, and is to be one of the characteristic forms of English verse down to Shakespeare's *Lucrece* (printed 1594). Although this stanza is used in French lyric before Chaucer, it cannot be doubted that his use of it in leisurely narrative is due to the similar stanza of Boccaccio in the originals of the two borrowed poems—the *ottava rima,* the chief narrative form of early Italian poetry, and later in English a favorite of Byron and Keats, and with the omission of its fifth line identical with Chaucer's stanza. What he owed most to Boccaccio was liberation. Poetry for him was an avocation from his means of livelihood, though an avocation essential to him, and with his fundamental modesty there might have been danger of his remaining too much under the influence of contemporary French poetry, then pretty much drifting in a backwater. For a good many years French and Boccaccian poetry guided him jointly, with-

in which Dr. Pratt found the Horace passage in a twelfth-century MS of John of Salisbury's *Policraticus,* and likewise from a fourteenth-century French translation of the *Policraticus.* Pratt, Robert A. "A Note on Chaucer's Lollius" *Modern Language Notes,* LXV, (1950), pp. 183-187.

out domination by either, and with increasing assertion of his own individuality.

For the *Troilus,* Boccaccio's *Filostrato* was the original and wholly essential. Boccaccio wrote it in order to show a woman how much she can make a man suffer through foiling his passion for her. His heroine, he shows us, in some degree represents Maria d'Aquino, supposed daughter of King Robert of Naples (and illegitimate like Boccaccio himself, and wife of a noble), whom he has pressed after, so far in vain (later not in vain). His hero's sufferings are his own. It was written probably in 1336, when the poet was nearly twenty-three, a more mature age in Italy and in the fourteenth century than now, but far less mature than Chaucer's when he was fascinated by the poem—as he might well be. It is impossible to see what Chaucer had in mind in writing his *Troilus,* and how it came to be what it is, without knowing the *Filostrato,* its virtues and limitations.

The matter of these poems of course does not come from the *Iliad,* unknown in the medieval West except in a late condensation, the "Ilias Latina." Indeed the *Iliad,* like the great Latin poets, like Virgil and Ovid, tells only episodes of the Troy-tradition, and the whole of this was known in the West only through two Latin prose translations from Greek, fictitiously ascribed to two eye-witnesses, Dictys and Dares, and dating from the fourth and the sixth centuries. With the renascence of classical culture in the twelfth century, the contents of these was put in the form inevitable then, a long (and very good) French poem by Benoit de Sainte-Maure. For the present purpose, the chief matter is that here first appear the loves of Troilus and Briseida, little developed, and doubtless invented by this poet in order to increase the love-interest. With the characteristic medieval veneration for so canonical a tale as that of Troy, Benoit's poem, including Troilus' love, was put back into Latin prose in 1287 by the Sicilian judge Guido de Columnis, and this and its numerous vernacular derivatives were the chief sources of modern acquaintance with the tradition of Troy down almost to the present day. To them is due the familiarity in everyday English, among those who have not a notion of what lies behind, of such words as myrmidon, Trojan, palladium, pander, to hector; the entire history is of intense interest, but irrelevant here. We are forced to return to Boccaccio, who to serve his own ends extracted and vastly developed Troilus' love-story, which more than anything else to the modern world has warmed and humanized the Troy-story, human as Homer is.

In the *Filostrato*, the situation and narrative though less extended than in the *Troilus* are identical. Criseida has been left in Troy by her traitor-father Calcas, rouses the love of Troilo in a temple during the festival of the Palladio, is induced by her cousin Pandaro to look on her lover favorably and very soon to surrender to him, and presently must be given up to the Greek besiegers in exchange for their Trojan prisoner Antenore. With all the simplicity of the narrative, there are two ingenious Chaucer-like incidents, in two ironical and lifelike situations. Just before Criseida leaves, certain Trojan ladies call on her to express congratulations and regret, and mistake her preoccupation and tears, due really to leaving Troilo, as due to leaving them; Boccaccio was no bad master for Chaucer. Again, when Troilo bids her farewell, he betrays his love for her to the hawk-eyed Diomede who has come to escort her to the Greek camp, and so stimulates his rivalry. The narrative proceeds as in Chaucer, with a speedy surrender by Criseida to Diomede. Within its limitations, the *Filostrato* is beautifully planned and executed. All that mars its good proportion is the immense and repetitious expression of emotion, especially grief and longing, but of this seemingly the Italian readers never wearied, and the emotional tone carries on the same general dispensation, the same fashion for dilating on feeling, exemplified in the *Book of the Duchess* and its forebears.

The people in the *Filostrato* are self-consistent, clean-cut, simple, because superficial. The young poet had no great insight or interest in human individualities, and the one

whom he portrays with most decision is the congenial Diomede, the skilful seducer, his skill needed less for persuasion
than to spare good manners and the lady's pride. Criseida is
self-consistent enough, attractive, superficial, rather artful and
thoroughly sensual; essentially as ardent and forward as
Troilo. Her portrait can hardly be called entirely flattering,
and must have been intended by the very vigorous author as
a warning as much as a compliment to his hoped-for para-
mour. Pandaro and Troilo are almost identical save in their
situation and its consequences, and embody the half-unreal
social ideal which the poet was concerned with. Its standards
are controlled by good taste alone, in no way by Catholic
morality; sincere sensual passion is sacred to Boccaccio; the
entire aim is "not to leave't undone but keep't unknown."
Pandaro plays the part of the friend-confidant usual in extended early love-stories, performs an essential and dramatic
function as an intriguer and as a sympathetic listener to the
lover's emotional outpourings; he is the most individual of
the persons, and the poet relished him. Troilo is the chief
vehicle of the emotion, which is what most interested the
poet, and is the kind of hero whom he usually depicted in
his younger years. We may take Boccaccio's word for it that
he is a mighty warrior, but what the poet cares about is not
his masculine pride and strength but his emotional and weak
moments. Women in Boccaccio's early works (though hardly
Criseida) are apt to dominate their men; they are queen-bees,
who wish men merely as males, though it is to be feared
hardly as fathers.

A few words should be said as to the conception of love
expressed in the *Filostrato,* and in a far more exquisite form
in the *Troilus;* something new in the world. It is not what is
called "amour courtois," "courtly love," in any sense which
gives that phrase value. By the eleventh century, society had
become stable enough to give women more power over men
who were willing to accept it; to give some freedom of action
to a vigorous *châtelaine* with a very likely uncongenial hus-

band, and with attractive young men who were attached to her large or small court and clever enough to see that success in life might be found by cultivating her favor—perhaps by the most obvious method, love-making. "Courtly love" fundamentally was a means adopted by ambitious and sensual young men to flatter patrician women. The classical exhibition of it is by Andreas Capellanus, of the later twelfth century, in his *De arte honeste amandi,* taken by moderns more seriously than by medievals. The essence of this love is the subjection of the man to the woman, in literature even to the point of his losing his wits when she is harsh with him; and this is a sensational element constantly recurring in romances, especially Arthurian, of the twelfth century and later. It might almost be said that to him emotional love is all, and to her little or nothing. Anyone of human perception who knows the Middle Ages knows that this conception merely embodies an ideal which appealed to patrician women and to some men as an escape from the brutal life of the time. The above analysis simplifies the reality. Undoubtedly many such love-affairs were very sincere and deeply felt, and produced such new creations as the *Vita Nuova* and Petrarch's sonnets which have refined the feeling of man toward woman for seven centuries, but we do not have to regard them as pictures of reality as much as expressions of imaginative ideal emotion, precious enough. "Courtly love" aided in the growth of romantic love, which has always existed but did not become articulate before the midst of the Middle Ages, and then became intensely so. This, and not "courtly love," is the climate of both the poems we are speaking of; in both, the primacy in enterprise and suffering is in the male, for such is the male's lot, but the woman does not tyrannize, and when things go wrong, in the *Troilus* at least, which is so much more human than the *Filostrato,* she suffers as much as he does. If the phrase "courtly love" has any useful meaning, neither poem is one of "courtly love," but of romantic and sensual love with elements of intense expression which the other had introduced to refine the sensual love which the Roman poets had written of. The *Troilus* is a poem of mutual romantic love with an intensity and concentration coupled with refinement which were then new in European poetry, and have rarely been paralleled since. Were it a poem merely of "courtly love," it would be far less good a poem. It is fundamental to understand that the moral standard accepted by Chaucer in the *Troilus,* whether or not thought of or lived up to, is that assumed in much of modern literature, not some bygone esoteric standard; the assumption is that sincere and intense physical passion if managed with good taste is honorable to both parties.

One thing more about this romantic love, its relation to marriage. Andrew the Chaplain pronounces his idea of love incompatible with marriage, and "courtly love" as I have described it is just that. But since the love in the two poems we are dealing with is of a different sort, inexperienced modern readers naturally ask why Criseyde and Troilus should not marry, and the answer is that if this were history there would be no reason. Many medieval love stories do end in marriage, and there would be no reason in medieval social prejudice why a royal prince should not marry a patrician subject, even with a discredited father and even in a doomed city. The answer is partly that fashionable readers found more interest and excitement in a furtive affair, and that what complexity there is in the very simple narrative results from the furtiveness. But the chief answer is this: To the medieval the most appealing narrative was historical, or at least traditional, between which two he felt little distinction; the imaginative poet would add much, and in minor matters might even contradict, but to change the essentials would have utterly confused his auditors—would have seemed to them nothing less than absurd, would have been completely rejected. This story was a familiar one, and its essence, its starting-point in the earliest versions, was Criseyde's infidelity. Nahum Tate's redramatizing *King Lear* in 1681 with a happy ending is now universally ridiculed, but there was better defence for that than there would have been for such treatment of Troilus' story.

Chaucer had never before read such a poem as the *Filostrato,* was utterly captivated and deeply moved by it, and began by following it closely. We cannot be sure how far he foresaw from the first his people and all their actions. But with his great human sympathy and perception, they as he found them grew under his fingers, and demanded more incident. Even though he cuts óut much of the emotional expression, especially of that from Troilus, the poem is nearly half as long again as the original and clearly lengthens much more than Chaucer intended, for the invocation at the beginning of the fourth book proves that that was expected to be the last book. The complexity and loveliness of his conception of Criseyde make the growth of love in her very gradual, and the second and most enchanting book is fullest of incident, mostly Chaucer's own extension of the story, which gives us the privilege of seeing this exquisite woman's emotions develop.

But the *Troilus* is not a poem of incident. It is a poem of people, their personalities and their feelings, and incident is only for their expression; as to just what this means we must allow ourselves a few words. One is not certain that one will be understood, or rather that what one says even if accepted at the moment will be coolly remembered by a reader of the poem who has surrendered to its illusion. (The difficulty in being cool with Chaucer's people is a great tribute to him; they are prone to break out into life.) But what is the ultimate reality of persons created by a poet's imagination? It is not the same as that of people who have really lived. In such people there were depths and unexpected peculiarities which may leave uncertain traces but may be guessed at, contradictory traits which leave us bewildered but may have to be accepted as due to unknown complexities. No such unknown traits should be postulated in characters created by a poet, for the ultimate reality of such characters is solely what was intended by the poet-creator; what he shows no sign of intending is not the reality, however attractive. It is true that one of Chaucer's usages is to include subtleties in characterization, hardly noticed at first, which accumulate to strengthen and enrich a personality which to a rapid reader seems only sketched. We shall meet again and again in the *Canterbury Tales* cases where a personality, though clear enough at first meeting, becomes more fully rounded out in such a way that we cannot doubt Chaucer intended this for those who have eyes to see. But actually contradictory traits, from a poet of Chaucer's imaginative insight and of his perception of his readers' reactions, should cause surprise, and they cannot be explained by unknown complexities of character which no one would otherwise infer.

All the chief people in the *Troilus* are rather highly individualized, far beyond the *Filostrato*; they are also refined beyond their originals, to fit what one may suppose a greater scrupulousness in English life, though not in fashionable reading. The proem of book II shows expectation of surprise in the auditors (seemingly even in the patrician auditors) at the procedure of the love-affair and especially at its furtiveness. There is likelihood that the modern reader will surrender eagerly to what entrances him, and disregard what troubles him. But trouble or not, there it all is to be accepted equally, and digested into what unity is possible. Chaucer was seized upon by the story, but could not help transcending it and developing it greatly, especially in the case of the heroine.

Diomede was simple for Chaucer, no subtlety of character needed; absolutely sure of himself, the most skilled seducer in all literature, and nothing else. Chaucer adapts him to the wholesome English by putting into his mouth the time-worn seducer's lie that he had never so courted a woman before, and was hers for life. These "wordes of the sodeyn Diomede," the momentum of his courtship, made Criseyde's prompt surrender easier. In her scenes with him she is infinitely pathetic. In soliloquy he reveals his egotism:

> But whoso myghte wynnen swich a flour
> From hym for whom she morneth nyght and day,
> He myghte seyn he were a conquerour.

Trojan men and women appear less worldly-wise than the Greek, as English rather than Italian we might say, which adds depth and feeling to the poem.

His extreme contrast with Troilus of course goes far to account for Criseyde's defection; women find confidence and social experience almost irresistible. Troilus would excite a woman's sympathy; in life, such a man might well win and hold some women through their maternal side, but Criseyde was too young to be content with this. Though in one or two scenes Troilus' youthful valor is very attractive, he is fundamentally unsure of himself with a woman. Unlike Troilo, he has never loved a woman before, but his contempt for lovers is plainly nothing but vanity and pose; and his emotional uncontrol and despair under trial are in reality those of an inexperienced man, and what we should call a neurotic. They function in the narrative simply to fulfil the ideal which pleased patrician women, and men who shared their taste. This is the reason for the exaggeration. From the very first line the subject is announced as his sorrows. Though other sides of him are touched on, it is without conviction. Repeatedly in the second book his judgment is sought and valued on practical matters. He is attractively modest about himself, including his own mental attainments, and therefore one may be surprised that latish in the fourth book he proves closely philosophical. Knowing that he must be separated from Criseyde for a season, in a highly lifelike resort to religion he visits a temple, and there he utters a very long and involved soliloquy derived from Boethius' *On the Consolation of Philosophy* and draws a fatalistic conclusion about human life. This Chaucer put in not in poetic heat, when he first wrote the *Troilus,* but when revising; though not in character the poet felt it impressive and harmonious with the hero's pessimistic frame of mind, reason enough for a medieval poet, and paralleled later in Chaucer. Though Troilus in gratitude for Pandarus' offered help offers to him any of his sisters married or unmarried, he dwells on his own emotion and not on sensuality. It is fairest to say that along with some moving insights in the portrayal of Troilus, he is sculptured in relief rather than in the round, in order to exhibit the kind of hero-in-love whom in Chaucer's younger days people liked to see; and that after Troilus' death his soul's blissful flight to the heavenly spheres and laughter at those who grieved for his death are the less incongruous. This passage, surprisingly like the soliloquy from Boethius, is likewise a late insertion, and not from the main source, but from Boccaccio's account of the flight of Arcita's soul in the *Teseide*. More than in any other of the persons the lifelike is sacrificed to the intense.

The confidant is the most lightly and unemotionally vivid of all the persons. Chaucer has changed him from cousin to uncle to Criseyde, probably in order to take some of the responsibility for what happens off her delicate shoulders, but a vivid scene in the second book as well as many other passages show that he is of Troilus' generation. Though no more a "courtly lover" than Troilus is, he is a sincere and suffering lover as everybody knows, but being more experienced and doubtless older he accepts his plight with much more manhood and outward cheerfulness. The part which the confidant plays in the story has always to the English world seemed so ignoble that he has given an ill-favored word to the language, but as for Chaucer's Pandarus with his eager vitality, his lightheartedness and humor and interest in other people, readers have not been too precise in noting what was done amiss as to morals or even honor. Without reading things into his picture in the way I have earlier deprecated, to the modern he is not only vivid but completely intelligible. He is extremely clever and adroit in word and act, loves to talk, is always in a hurry and runs and leaps. His motives for playing his part in what happens are manifold; the chief are that he is thoroughly good-natured and warm-hearted, is totally without moral scruples, and truly believes he is doing an unmixed service to both his friend and his blighted and widowed niece; above all that he functions at his best in intrigue, for he is a born intriguer and the father of it.

Criseyde is far less simple, and less clear to some moderns, but few will cavil if she is called one of the most attractive women in all imaginative literature; so much so that one may be allowed to protest at calling her by the name of Shakespeare's Cressida, who by reason of the changes in the story through two centuries has become unutterably cheapened. Criseyde is Chaucer's lady; Criseyde let her remain, as Chaucer felt her in some of the tenderest and most masculine lines he ever wrote:

> Ne me ne list this sely womman chyde
> Forther than the storye wol devyse.
> Hire name, allas! is punysshed so wide,
> That for hire gilt it oughte ynough suffise.
> And if I myghte excuse hire any wise,
> For she so sory was for hire untrouthe,
> Iwis, I wolde excuse hire yet for routhe.

Till near the end she is Chaucer's own creation, learned about by us as we learn about our friends, through her words and acts, not from analytic statements. With delicate finesse we are shown her clearly as seen by Troilus, Diomede, herself, and indeed others. Even in the *Canterbury Tales* no one is so fully pictured by such means, though in some of the *Tales* such methods are used. Clearly her original had taken hold on Chaucer, and gestated within him into a rounded and many-sided person. In this earliest portrait of a lady in English literature, she perceives in any circumstances what conduct and attitude are fitting however trying the circumstances may be; keeps her head, is critical and perceptive, highly intelligent, at times analytic and intellectual, does not surrender to her emotions till her judgment approves, having a wonderful balance of feeling and good sense. There are fifty allusions and quotations one would like to make. There is great pathos in so young and lovely a woman so cruelly placed, unprotected, even suspect, that she is forced to beware whither the currents may carry her. Though she has been married, she has not love on her mind, and we are justified in fancying that she had never been roused by her husband—very likely as so often in patrician marriage far older than she. In one of the most exquisite of scenes, about the middle of book II, she asks her friends about love, and herself muses and dreams about it as of something perilous and unknown. In her circumstances till lately evidently nothing has ever forced her to be wary or combative; the only trait that in the least prepares us for her undoing is her softness—softness is the word, and together with tenderness it is her most endearing trait. Her love and suffering for Troilus though less dwelt on are as great as his. Her softness is nothing like an amorousness which would account or prepare for her infidelity, which the unprejudiced modern reader rebels against. Half through the final book, still the same tender Criseyde, she grows pale and thin with longing. Thus far she has grown under Chaucer's matchless intuition; in every touch she is sweet, loving, and essentially good. Chaucer feels no obligation to unify her first state with her last, but he concentrates his imagination in surrender to the first.

But the poet can no longer defer what must happen in the familiar story, and here he adopts a strange and highly medieval expedient as in the *Book of the Duchess*—he describes her in detail and analyzes her character by items,

Tendre-herted, slydynge of corage.

At first sight this passage of three full stanzas, suitable for introducing Criseyde, is a strange interruption at this point, but a sharp look will reveal the explanation. It is preceded by a similar stanza about Diomede (in Boccaccio), and followed by two about Troilus (Chaucer's addition). Chaucer

was conscious that he had reached the great conflict of the
whole poem, within Criseyde, and between the pull of the
two men, also conscious perhaps that he had in no way
prepared for it, as in good truth he had not. Her susceptibility and unsteadiness are the explanation, but mentioned late
and crudely here. Diomede has just formed his resolution to
attempt her, and the poet describes his powerful masculinity;
then Criseyde's bodily attractiveness, but ending with her
sweetest moral qualities, her sympathy for others, and her
softness—and baldly states her susceptibility and unsteadiness, which she had not shown earlier. Troilus' virtues follow, but with masculinity less vivid than Diomede's. When
that was about to begin which everyone knew must happen,
Chaucer with curious directness tells us why it happened.
The passage comes here because here is where Diomede begins to operate, and here therefore Boccaccio describes his at-
tractions. But in *Filostrato* the other two are sufficiently clear
and consistent already, not so in *Troilus*. Chaucer therefore
looked up earlier versions of the story and there got more
or less of the detail here. But he does not make the dramatic
most of the constrasts, nor much emphasize Criseyde's susceptibility and instability, but rather as earlier her sweetness.

On the tenth day after her coming, Diomede begins his
skilful siege of her, and is welcomed with merely hospitable
good manners; but progress is fast; even in her deep sadness
he is promised a meeting the next day and at any time, without resistance, and not without other very encouraging hints.
After the day spent with her, he is allowed to depart with her
glove as token. That night she begins to think of him seriously; and the following day, not certainly but according to
the plain implication,

> He refte hire of the grete of al hire peyne.

When it was that she made other minor concessions, for one
of which the poet reproaches her ("and that was litel
nede"), we are not told; nor when it was that in her own

mind she takes her pathetic farewell of Troilus,

> And gilteles, I woot wel, I yow leve.
> But al shal passe; and thus take I my leve;

nor when she makes the last surrender. But her defection began the tenth day, the day ironically when she had promised to return to Troy, and the poet does little to mitigate its speed.

Hereafter we see her no more. The poet has not the heart to watch the steps of her decline. We merely hear of her through insincere but piteous letters to Troilus, the last of them full of unfair reproaches. If she were a real person all this disclosure of hidden fundamental weakness might have happened, but any witness of it would be as much surprised as most modern readers are apt to be dissatisfied with the successive glimpses which are all the poet allows. I must repeat that, in an imagined person, there are no traits which the creator does not disclose. How shall we explain Chaucer's procedure with Criseyde? The Italian Criseide is attractive, and he took deep pleasure in transforming her into a far more attractive Englishwoman, but when she came to her end in the traditional story, of course, she had to do just as her original had done. We are left to draw the inference that no matter how sweet and good any woman may be she cannot be trusted. Whether or not Chaucer believed this all his life, it was good medieval psychology. This may well be the reason why neither he nor his early readers seem to have been as troubled by the discord as is the modern reader.

The epilogue of the poem is also unprepared for, but follows well enough from this inference. Chaucer, with heartfelt sincerity, renounces the pagans and all their works, bids "yonge fresshe folkes, he or she," turn from worldly feigned loves to love of Jesus Christ, and ends with an imposing invocation of the Holy Trinity. After the tale had begun it beguiled the poet more and more, but the inevitable ending, forced on him by the inexorable tradition, not by any inexorable destiny, more and more alienated him, till Christian

asceticism swallowed him up. If the exquisite loves of Criseyde
and Troilus end in sorrow, there must be nothing in sensual
love, Chaucer seems to say. The strangeness of the poem is
quite intelligible, and perhaps makes us like Chaucer the
better. But assuredly he wrote at the end of a literary dispensation. To live in the full beauty of the poem, one must
completely surrender to Chaucer's own momentum at every
point.

All these people have one trait in common, they are
aristocrats, are free from sordid care, know the code, and in
minor matters go right by instinct. Some of the lesser persons are unerring sketches of patricians, especially Helen,
Hector, Deiphebus, and Antigone, and there is no bourgeois.
Nowhere else in Chaucer is there so intimate a picture of
patricians. The style fits, almost throughout on a level of
literary dignity rare in Chaucer; some passages are even
stately. It is not to be supposed for an instant that in the
decorative element he plodded into a deliberate following of
the precepts of medieval authorities on rhetoric; though
doubtless aware of them, he spontaneously admired the manner of Boccaccio, the ancients and their other followers, who
were the exemplars of the exalted style of which he was in
the vein here. In style as in tone, he scarcely ever attempted
the same thing again. Had Criseyde not so fascinated him,
perhaps he would not have cultivated it here. The superla-
tive merits of the *Canterbury Tales* are very different. The
Troilus is one of his greatest poems, but far from being characteristic.

It would aid in understanding the *Troilus,* assuredly in
understanding Chaucer, to know in which stage in his development he wrote it, though the order in which he wrote
his poems is not a matter of the first importance. It has never
been certainly determined or agreed on, partly because his
poetry was wholly apart from his daily life, so active and
varied, and therefore contains few allusions to concrete affairs. It is full of the experience he was learning from this

life, but is nearly devoid of reliable allusions to specific incidents. This fact has piqued scholars in their matter-of-fact
moments. In many of his works they have for years continual-
ly been recognizing such allusions, without always convincing
each other. In the *Troilus* some have seen an allusion to an
astronomical situation, the conjunction of the planets Jupiter
and Saturn in the sign Cancer, in 1385, and have taken that
date as the *terminus a quo*. But the implied crowding of
Chaucer's writing about this time is hard to accept. Further,
the situation was so rare and so important astrologically that
it would have been foreseen years before by the astrologically-
minded, as Chaucer was even more than most medievals. A
watcher of the skies would for years have seen Jupiter slowly
overhauling Saturn toward Cancer, and have speculated as to
human consequences when they met. A fancied allusion to
King Richard's wife Anne in Criseyde standing matchless in
beauty,

Right as oure firste letter is now an A,

is disposed of when one thinks of the beauty of an illumi-
nated initial when books were scarce, when one might walk
London from end to end and never see a letter from A to Z,
and when illumination was one of the chief forms of art.
Comparison of a lady to a beautifully formed manuscript
letter leading the alphabet and adorned with glowing gold-
leaf and with that matchless blue is highly pleasing even today, and in Chaucer's day would not be prosaic or banal. Still
more improbable is any allusion to the uproarious peasant-
revolt of 1381 early in book IV, for the uproar in favor
of exchanging Criseyde for Antenor is not among the Trojan
rabble but in parliament. Obviously none of the above explains any difficulty; it merely undertakes to recognize allusions in passages perfectly natural without allusions. Chaucer
chronology involves what might be called a set of variables
depending on each other; of several other poems whose uncertain dates are involved here two are the *House of Fame*
and the *Palamon and Arcite,* the first version of the *Knight's*

Tale, which we shall find some reason to date after the *Troilus.* Undoubtedly the reason why so many scholars have been disposed to think the *Troilus* relatively late is its power and beauty; many find it hard to believe that after writing it Chaucer wrote some other poems which we like so much less because so much less congenial to us. But no one can pronounce as to whether such a poem as the *Troilus* was more likely from Chaucer in the mid-thirties or the mid-forties, especially since the aim, tone, and spirit are so very unlike anything else he ever wrote.

Other matters incline others to an early date. Some have felt substantial reason to believe the poem was written (or at least was known of and well under way) before 1377, the approximate date of what looks like an allusion to it in the *Mirour de l'Omme,* the long French poem of Chaucer's friend John Gower, in which a man asleep in church dreams he hears

> chanter la geste
> De Troylus et de la belle
> Creseide.

The name of Troilus' mistress begins with a C only in Chaucer and Boccaccio, whom Gower would have known only through Chaucer. There is some, though far from conclusive indication of an early date, or at least against a very late date, in the fact that in 1387 Thomas Usk's *Testament of Love* names and quotes the poem, not in the original but in a revised version. And finally Chaucer's disciple John Lydgate, who knew much about Chaucer and his works, tells us that he wrote *Troilus* "longe or that he deyde," and "in youthe." None of this evidence is by any means conclusive, but to some it looks more that way than the evidence touched on above for a late date. Also, various points have been noted in this chapter which seem to suggest a writer immensely endowed but inexperienced. And no one will deny that a man like Chaucer could write a poem like the *Troilus* in the mid-thirties.

CHAPTER FOUR

ANELIDA AND ARCITE

NO FEATURE of Chaucer's literary life is more noticeable than the number of works he left unfinished. Writing for him was pure avocation, though doubtless essential
to him; he made his living otherwise, and no doubt many
people did not think of him as a writer at all. Writing largely
in shreds and patches of time, it is not surprising that he
should find a delayed enterprise losing its savor for him, or
else that a new idea should irresistibly distract him by stimulating his imagination afresh. He was specially apt to drop
poems which we may well believe were original in idea or
matter; he invented his plots little more than Shakespeare
did. If mere ingenuity were a first-rate literary gift, Sir Arthur
Conan Doyle who has delighted so many tired readers would
be one of the greatest of writers. Such poems are the *Anelida
and Arcite*, the *House of Fame*, the *Tales* of the *Cook* and
the *Squire*, to say nothing of several less original unfinished
works; the only one of his finished narratives to which no
close parallels has been found, though its contents may be
due to hearsay, is the *Canon's Yeoman's Tale*. The fact that
the plots of all of the unfinished poems seem to be original
favors the view that their incompleteness is not due to any
loss of endings early in the manuscript tradition, especially
since there are a considerable number of independent early
authorities for the texts of all of them.

The *Anelida and Arcite* is the antithesis of the *Troilus*. It is evident in the prologue of the *Legend of Good Women* that Chaucer was open to reproach, light or serious, for writing discouragingly in the *Troilus* about women's fidelity. In the Anelida on the contrary, he wrote of a man faithless to a beautiful and suffering woman, a man who like Criseyde in her second letter tries to conceal his own treachery. This poem like the other was meant to be read aloud, and one can fancy light approval at hearing the lines,

> Or what man mighte within the chambre dwelle,
> If I to him rehersen sholde the helle
> That suffreth fair Anelida the quene.

The same general situation of a cruel inconstant male appears also in the *Squire's Tale* and early in the *House of Fame* as well, as in Ovid. Anelida submits to Arcite as Troilus to Criseyde, and indeed the same moral might be drawn from both poems, that in both man and woman emotional dignity is essential to enduring love, a moral congenial to Chaucer.

The plot, what there is of it, is so elementary that there is no need to seek a source for it. Some elements and passages are drawn from the *Teseide*, Boccaccio's other long poem, fine and highly original in manner. It would be natural that Chaucer should interest himself in this as a complement to the shorter and more intense *Filostrato*. The *Anelida* may well be the earliest of his four poems—the others are the *Troilus,* the *Parliament of Fowls,* and the *Knight's Tale*—which, to variable extent and in very different ways, show influence and use of the *Teseide*. The chief sign of this influence in *Anelida* is the name of Arcite, taken from the most attractive person in the *Teseide*. Another is the abrupt ending when Chaucer announces a description of the temple of Mars; this suggests that he intended to borrow from the *Teseide* the imposing description which so stands out in the *Knight's Tale*. He uses also, and quotes in Latin, Statius' *Thebaid*, as he acknowledges at the beginning,

> First folowe I Stace, and after him Corynne.

This is the usual bespeaking of confidence by citing early writers. No identification of the second has ever been established, and even if Corinna was not merely chosen for the rhyme, she is probably no more authentic here than Lollius is in the *Troilus*.

The *Anelida* leaves us wondering what the poet was aiming at and working toward. The attempts made by scholars to take it as symbolical of certain contemporary social situations or scandals have been less successful than with the *Parliament* and *Legend*, and have not found favor. Certainly no such explanation is called for here as with them. We are puzzled. The martial opening of the invocation at the beginning is hardly justified by the opening of the narrative at Theseus' triumph after his military victory, nor by Anelida's visit to the temple of Mars at the end, though none can say what events might have followed or what the lovelorn lady is doing there. So unattractive a man as Arcite can hardly be intended to be the hero of a later military adventure. The promised subject, actual subject so far as the poem extends, is the love affairs of the titular pair. The most memorable feature in the entire fragment is Anelida's "Complaint" at the end, forming more than a third of the poem. It is in the contemporary French manner, and with its complicated symmetry, internal rhyme and the like, is one of the most technically elaborate things Chaucer ever wrote.

A possible explanation of the genesis of the *Anelida* is suggested by comparison with the *Complaint of Mars*, this also beginning with a proem and a very simple narrative, leading to and ending with an elaborate "Complaint," about half of the whole poem, not unlike that in the *Anelida*, though less elaborate. Chaucer may have begun the *Anelida* with the intention of combining an elaborate lyric with an extensive framing narrative, using some of the very unlike and very impressive matter which he found in the *Teseide*. Of this the most notable is the description of the temple of Mars, before which the poet fetches up at the very end of the fragment. He may have come to feel that the fine *Teseide* was worthy of a better use than that of mere bits or portions in the nondescript *Anelida*. There may have immediately followed in his literary biography the *Palamon and Arcite* (perhaps also unfinished and therefore unpolished), the first form of the *Knight's Tale*. That the *Anelida* preceded both of these is indicated by his selecting the more attractive of their heroes to lend his name to the rascally lover in the *Anelida*. Of course all this is mere conjecture, and may imply that he began this poem with no very clear idea what it was to contain. Chaucer was a versatile poet, but as we know not inventive in plot, and one should be prepared for experiments, not all carried through with success. The original character of the story, an inversion of the usual love-story, and the technical virtuosity of the lyric would account for its finding the favor shown by the considerable number of early copies.

CHAPTER FIVE

THE HOUSE OF FAME

THE *House of Fame,* like the *Anelida,* is one of Chaucer's unfinished poems, and may be called experimental. Unlike the *Anelida* it is an experiment, not in the formal, stately, and emotional, but in the casual and easy-going, more congenial to Chaucer. But he never elsewhere tried anything like this poem. Though full of wide literary reminiscences, it has no chief source and fully belongs in no one category.

Like the *Duchess,* though less so, it follows the usages and manner of the well-defined, fashionable, and quite contemporary French type of poem, the love-vision, from the thirteenth-century *Roman de la Rose* to Froissart's *Paradys d'Amour.* For one thing, the *Book of the Duchess* and the *House of Fame* are the only two of Chaucer's poems which adopt the form of verse which that generally uses, the eight-syllable couplet, easy and simple and light, adapted to chatting about one's own affairs; yet with the disadvantage that the thick-falling rimes overemphasize the jingling form, especially with the diffuseness of Middle English words and style; eight syllables convey less meaning than in Walter Scott. Like other love-visions, the *House of Fame* is in the form of a dream which gives lifelike freedom for rambling and inconsequence, more notable in this poem than elsewhere in Chaucer; like others it gives the date of the dream—but it is the tenth day of December, not spring-time, preparing us for a different spirit. Among many resemblances to love-visions is the presence, in the first and third books, of the elaborate temples of Venus and of Fame. Though the descriptions owe something to Ovid and Virgil, and though such edifices are not uncommon in medieval narrative, Chaucer, like his fellow-poets, pictured them in his own mind as similar to medieval churches, with pinnacles, tabernacles and images in niches — not before modern times had people much idea what classical times actually looked like. As in other love-visions, there is the fanciful adornment which comes from personification and ancient mythology. Chaucer's consciousness that he is in the stream of the love-vision appears in the constant touching on love, flirting with the subject and skirting it, but obviously with no deep interest in it, or clear intention of actually entering on it, and indeed, as so often, disowning knowledge of love. Even at the end, love is only one of very many subjects of the gossip in the house of twigs, but without suggestion of leading up to some special interest, or of the refined, mythological, fanciful treatment of love in polite poetry, suggesting rather love and marriage in actual daily life and irresponsible gossip. It is no more fair to say that the *House of Fame* is primarily a poem of love than an autobiographical allegory or a parody of the *Divine Comedy*. A striking but unfair case can be made out for any of these theories by picking out seemingly favorable evidence and disregarding all else and all proportion. Chaucer's poems have often been misinterpreted thus.

In spite of the independence and originality, hardly any of Chaucer's poems show so many reminiscences from earlier works, or at least resemblances to them, in Italian, French, and Latin, as memories flashed to mind. What has drawn most attention is the familiarity shown with Dante's *Divine Comedy*. Nothing is more noteworthy in the poem than its interest and learning in science, astronomy and especially physics and the principles of sound. Such interests appearing throughout his poems are a characteristic combined result of

Chaucer's rationality and his interest in things as they are. For such information here, he seems to draw not only on the *Roman de la Rose* but on Cicero's *Somnium Scipionis*, on Boethius, on Alanus de Insulis and other medieval Latin writers as well as upon common knowledge.

More surprising, in the first book there is a long summary of Virgil's *Aeneid*. In an unrealistic conception of carving, its whole narrative is sculptured on the walls of a superb glass temple of Venus. This is irrelevant to the actual and promised subject of the poem; the highlighting of the Dido-Aeneas love story is due no more to the love-vision frame than to its intrinsic interest. It is followed by mentions of other faithless males, a foretaste of the *Legend of Good Women* in making amends for the record of Criseyde's infidelity. All this, hundreds of lines, is like the long beginnings of the *Book of the Duchess* and the *Parliament of Fowls* in having little appropriateness but much decorative force and a great deal of intrinsic value in that it introduced ill-read auditors to the distinguished *Aeneid*, to Ovid's *Metamorphoses* and Cicero's *Somnium Scipionis*. The lighter literature of the Middle Ages did not highly value unity; modern literature has learned its value from the ancients, and from the drama, in which concentration adds so much to power. But one can imagine that listening patrician ladies and men, not Latin-readers but ambitious and active-minded, would welcome such alert introductions by a vivacious poet with a reputation for reading. At least they would gain a nodding acquaintance with works often referred to by their intellectual betters.

Besides all this, literature both popular and otherwise, folklore, and actual life have left their impress here and there; the poet's imagination got its fuel from everywhere. The extraordinary house of news and gossip, flimsily built of basket-work, recalls peasants' houses of the time in Ireland and Britain. Its fantastic whirling and access only with difficulty and with the aid of the eagle, a "helpful animal," are paralleled chiefly in semi-popular tradition and poem. The poet carried up by an eagle may be reminiscent of Dante, or of Ganymede in Ovid or Virgil; it was also widely believed among the Syrians and Romans that the spirits of the dead might be carried to the sky on the back (not in the claws) of an eagle. It is a well-stored tradition and memory indeed which has formed the *House of Fame*.

So far as the poem shows concentrated aim toward any goal it is in the latter half and more, an original, decorative symbolic picture of celebrity and gossip, and their caprices and untrustworthiness. Undefined and wandering as this often is, what precedes is still more undefined and motiveless, save for decorative imagination. After the temple of Venus, with its summary of the *Aeneid*, the poet finds himself in a desert; whence an eagle carries him afar up, with much discourse upon the constitution of the universe, and also upon the poet's situation in life, both irrelevant to the subject of love. Fame, whose house he has now reached, has for the most part the Latin significance of report, rumor, gossip, but when he reaches and especially when he enters her house, he conceives of her in the narrower sense of celebrity, renown, which is much the same thing. The purpose of this is decorative and satirical. He gives not only a list of the great literary names of antiquity but an imposing scene with the statues of these worthies on pedestals. With the medievals' filial feeling toward antiquity they never tired of this sort of list. The goddess Fame's unreliability is well indicated by her variation in stature and the variation in the size of the House. The chief satire on the caprices of celebrity (as of Fortune in other medieval poetry) comes next, when some nine groups of people enter asking for good repute, or for obscurity, or even for ill repute, and are granted and refused through the goddess Fame's whim, with little regard for justice. This is one of the most original and pointed scenes in the poem. And another such follows, in the visit to the House of Rumor, which had been promised early in the second book. But Fame has almost throughout the wide sense of report, the writers who are

memorialized by statue are those who wrote of great events
and heroes in antiquity, and it is musicians and singers as
conveying report that for the most part produce near the
beginning of the third book the charming picture of gleemen
and buglers:

> And many flowte and liltyng horn,
> And pipes made of grene corn,
> As han thise lytel herde-gromes,
> That kepen bestis in the bromes.

One thing illogically leads to another; musicians to jugglers,
and they to sorceresses, and they to natural magic. Throughout Chaucer lets his fancy go, and we shall delude ourselves
if at any point we think that *now* he has reached his main
path. The casualness of all which precedes prepares us for the
vagueness of the manner in which the fragment breaks off—
in the confusion of the House of Rumor there appears "a man
of gret auctorite." But of who he is and what he is to do
we have no hint. The absence of any concentrated aim for the
poem is shown not only by its growth over and over again
by casual and often inappropriate associations, but by the
invocation of the third book,

> This lytel laste bok thou gye!

Clearly the third book was to end the poem, just as the
Troilus was to have ended with its fourth. Now book one contains 508 lines, book two 582, but the third breaks off incon-
clusively after no less than 1068 lines. What Chaucer would
have done had the spirit moved him to continue it is useless
to guess (though this has often been done), but all goes to
show that his motive was amusement of a sportive fancy.
Whatever idea he started the poem with and recurred to,
when he named it the *House of Fame,* as he did himself in the
prologue of the *Legend of Good Women* and the *Retractions,*
he thought not of a love-vision but of the most original feature at the end of the poem, the imaginations conveyed by

shipmen and pilgrims—

> Wynged wondres faste fleen.

Why he should have intended such a poem we can guess. One of the most noticeable passages is the one early in the second book in which the eagle carrying him speaks of Jupiter's compassion for his life—returning as he does from his toilsome reckonings at the custom-house, and instead of sociability sitting with his nose in another book. Whether or not this is a fair picture of Chaucer's life at any time, it suggests a frame of mind which would relish giving a loose to inventive fancy. That is just what the poem does. Freedom, letting himself go, is what marks off this poem from everything else he ever wrote.

In one matter of freedom especially the poem is unique, that is in open though modest self-revelation, rare in medieval poetry, and voiced chiefly through the most characteristic figure, the eagle, probably the earliest of Chaucer's mock-heroic, humanized animals. Normally so stately and heraldic, this bird here is actually chummy. The passage just mentioned about Chaucer's hermit-like life,

> Although thyn abstynence ys lyte,

gives not the only such revelation. The chummy eagle calls him by his name,

> Geffrey, thou wost ryght wel this;

and also, though belittling the force of his wits and his small success in love (as the poet so often does more directly of himself), observes his fertility in writing of love; also lightly. The expression of a jocular mood shows even in the eagle's account of how human talk spreads in waves to the distant house of Fame:

> And whoso seyth of trouthe I varye,
> Bid hym proven the contrarye.

(This from the scientific-minded Chaucer!)

> Take yt in ernest or in game.

Mention of the "ducat in Venyse" brings the light personal line,

> Of which to lite al in my pouche is.

The most startling personal allusion comes near the beginning of book II. To the dazed poet hanging from his claws, the eagle cries,

> "Awak," . . . .
> Ryght in the same vois and stevene
> That useth oon I koude nevene;
> And with that vois, soth for to seyn,
> My mynde cam to me ageyn,
> For hyt was goodly seyd to me,
> So nas hyt never wont to be.

Whose can this shrewish voice be but Mistress Philippa Chaucer's? If the poet had not meant his own wife he would have had too much perceptive foresight to write such lines which would assuredly be so understood. Never mind at this point about any suggestions as to his wife's personality or his marital relations. Here he was letting himself go; not perhaps with good taste, but the fourteenth century was more hard-boiled than the twentieth. The groups of people begging for fame lead to one of the fine and manful personal passages; asked if he has come to beg for fame, he replies,

> Sufficeth me, as I were ded,
> That no wight have my name in honde.
> I wot myself best how y stonde;
> For what I drye, or what I thynke,
> I wil myselven al hyt drynke.

Another personal touch to mention is in the invocation to book III, where he shows complete consciousness of his own literary style. May Apollo guide "this lytel laste bok"! It is not to be art poetical, but the rime "lyght and lewed," somewhat agreeable,

> Though som vers fayle in a sillable.

Chaucer was quite aware of his own carelessness about nine-syllable lines (and seven-syllable lines). The poem does not aspire to the occasional ambitious manner of the *Troilus* and the *Anelida*. He is conscious that the verse is even more irregular than that of the short couplets of the French love-visions that started him off. "Lewd," popular, means that he surrenders also to English verse which partly carries on old English traditional style in rhythm. Again he is letting himself go, as to his style, as much as about personal affairs.

This free informality bears on the time in his life when he wrote the *House of Fame*. While in the same verse as the *Book of the Duchess,* in manner and spirit this poem differs from it almost as much as does the *Troilus,* so much that it is as easy to believe it later than the *Troilus* and the *Anelida* as to believe it earlier. If Chaucer wished to let his fancy go "for fun" at any time in mid-life, he might well have written such a poem as the *House of Fame*. The short couplet assuredly suits its spirit and intention, and might be revived by him at any time. It fits the emancipated spirit of the poem which, rare because it is in the Middle Ages, suggests experience, and which shows nowhere more than in the light touch with which this poem handles its learning and wide reading. Its lightness and characteristically Chaucerian humor, while not making it nearly so fine a poem as the *Troilus,* allows us to call it quite as mature. In an age of literary conventionality, it was a very mature man who had the courage to forsake seriousness. There is no clear evidence for any date more precise than after 1374, when he undertook at the custom-house the "rekenynges" which he tells us so staled his spirit, and before 1385, when he was allowed the relief of a deputy to keep the records. But there are two lines close together which though some critics may dissent, seem to others to point to a time after the writing of the *Troilus*. Toward the middle of the third book, among the authorities on the Trojan war, are

> he Lollius,
> And Guydo eke de Columpnis,
> And Englyssh Gaufride eke, ywis.

Lollius is twice mentioned in the *Troilus* as the feigned author of its original. As remarked in Chapter III, Lollius is not a name for Boccaccio who is ignored because a vernacular, recent, and little known writer without authority. Medieval readers liked to be told of an impressive ancient or early source for what they read, without necessarily believing in its authenticity much more than moderns have believed in Gulliver. It is true that medievals more than moderns did not fully discriminate between history and fiction, but then as now there was sometimes between author and reader a tacit agreement to accept a feigned authenticity. If Chaucer had lately written the *Troilus* all is clear as to why Lollius appears in the *House of Fame* as a writer on Troy; Chaucer here is confirming the feigned authenticity of the *Troilus*. And there is something still more curious. Just after Guido, author of the most-read account of Troilus and Criseyde and of the whole Troy-story, appears "English Geoffrey" as another authority on Troy. This has usually been taken as Geoffrey of Monmouth. But he is British-Celtic, and strongly anti-English; Chaucer might not have scrupled to make him turn in his grave, but why not have named him "Britoun Gaufride," if named at all? But this is the chief surprise: Geoffrey's *Historia Regum Britanniae* does not tell the story of Troy, but that of some of its refugees, practically starting with Aeneas' descendants. A few hundred lines earlier the sociable eagle had called to Chaucer by his name, "Geoffrey." It would harmonize with the humor and intimacy of the poem if "English Geoffrey" is the author of the *Troilus* himself! Such personal allusions as these, if here correctly interpreted, as well as those earlier mentioned, together with the slowness of the poem in getting under way, and its specially marked tendency to digress, and the prolongation of the final book, and its very inconclusive breaking-off, all justify doubt whether the *House of Fame* was begun with any clean-cut purpose or meaning, except irresponsibly "for fun."

CHAPTER SIX

THE PARLIAMENT OF FOWLS

THE *Parliament* of Fowls also is in the pattern of the love-vision. It is less superficial, far richer, than the *House of Fame*—one of the richest poems Chaucer ever wrote, far advanced in maturity; yet like *Fame* more expressive of himself on various sides than of the mere literary tradition of love which was thriving among the fashionable. It begins with avowing allegiance to love, which as so often he disclaims knowing save through books. With his usual tact this bourgeois man, not physically alluring, is heading off personal chaff; but it is quite clear that attractive young patricians who had love on their minds attracted him. As usual he is in a main current, but swims his own independent course in it; far from indifferent to his own day, he nevertheless maintains his own individual momentum.

After indicating that love is to be his subject, he turns to his reading, which proves to have nothing to do with love, but is none the worse for that, being Cicero's *Somnium Scipionis,* one of the grandest and most Christian and human things which have come down from antiquity. The medievals, with their veneration for the classics from which they were conscious of learning everything except Christianity, responded gratefully to such likenesses to their religion as they found among the classical stories—in the *Somnium,* the connection between man's devotion to morals and to the common good and his eternal destiny in the heavens. In the *Duchess* the poet's reading about the loving wife Alcyone, which helps him to sleep, prepares for the dream of the loving Blanche; in *Fame* there is less relevance in the survey of the *Aeneid;* in the *Parliament* the only fitness in the reading is that it ends in sleep and supplies Africanus as the conductor into the garden of love. Here more clearly than in these other poems, the classic narrative is used as introduction not because of any bearing on the contents of the rest of the poem but for its own splendor, also perhaps to lend dignity; at any rate this is what it does in high degree.

That it should be the task of a Roman soldier to take the dreamer to the garden of love, composed largely of memories of the *Roman de la Rose* and of Boccaccio's *Teseide,* is a typical illustration of the mingling of classical memories with the decorative and superficially emotional that makes the charm of fashionable literature in Chaucer's day. The profuse ancient mythology, of course, is one of the habitual love-vision elements. Once again he disclaims any personal experience of love. He is not here thinking of profound emotional love (to which, as one of the strongest things in life, he had so surrendered his imagination in the *Troilus),* but of the fanciful conception which the fashionable adopted for fun, or else as a graceful cloak for sensuality. Chaucer's tacit acceptance of sensual love in this poem is shown by the sensual deity Priapus "in sovereyn place" in love's temple; the worldliness is shown by Venus' porter being Richesse, which is constantly paralleled in earlier writers. The lover must recommend himself by costly presents rather than by deep feeling; Richesse indicates even more worldliness than Love's porter, Idleness, in the *Romaunt of the Rose.* The Middle Ages are middle indeed when Scipio Africanus is accepted as introducing Chaucer to the pretty garden of sensual and worldly love!

The charm of the description is largely in harmonious literary reminiscence, stimulating to the well-read memory, to one who knows not only Dante or Boccaccio, but also Ovid and other Latin poets. These last spring to mind when one reads the lists of trees and birds each with a poetic epithet; with "the boxtre pipere," "the saylynge fyr," "the dronke vyne," Chaucer is less borrowing than prolonging the life of a convention, to the keen pleasure of the well-read. Like the use of the *Somnium Scipionis,* this contributes to the unique richness of the poem. The garden, together with its fullness of literary reminiscence, has the also Chaucerian charm of smiling observation of animals, and especially little animals, "smale fishes lighte, with fynnes rede," 'bestes smale of gentil kynde," "the litel conyes to here pley gonne hye." The smiling scrutiny of animals was clearly one of Chaucer's habits, and it draws modern sympathy. Indeed the characterizing of the bird-lovers later in the *Parliament* is its trait which is most likely to flash to mind when one thinks of the poem. The chatty and well-informed eagle in the *House of Fame* has pre- pared us not only for the immortal feathered married couple Chantecleer and Pertelote in the *Nun's Priest's Tale* but for the feathered cross-section of humanity in the *Parliament.*

Though this is a love-poem its "emperesse" is not Venus but the "noble goddesse Nature," which rather appeals to the naturalistically-minded modern. Sex-life, and the sentiment with which man has beautified it, are not often in the Middle Ages accepted as part of the utilitarian course of nature. The vehicles here of sex-love, birds, are fitting for their conspi- cuous love-making every spring-time, as well as their inex- haustible charm and their conspicuousness in the poetry with which the *Parliament* belongs. This is doubtless why they were chosen rather than any weakness of Chaucer's for St. Valentine's day, on which the poem is placed and when in moderate climates birds were supposed to choose their mates for the year. On this day also are placed the *Complaint of Mars* and the probably genuine *Complaynt d'Amours.* The poet himself tells us that Nature encompassed by birds is derived from Alanus de Insulis' twelfth-century *De Planctu*

Naturae; this is a frigid, ingenious, and learned poem attacking here and there the vice of homosexuality and like perversions. The vice as existing peeps out occasionally in medieval books, but never in Chaucer save in a hint with the Summoner and the Pardoner in the *Canterbury Tales* and an allusion in the *Parson's Tale.* Of all great English poets none is more balanced and normal than Chaucer. With Nature and her birds, he improves on Alanus (in whom they are merely depicted on her robe along with fish and beasts) by showing them congregated and debating about her in the flesh. Indeed he owes very little to Alanus, a monstrosity of rambling paradox and artificiality, for the assembly and debating of birds appears a good many times elsewhere in medieval literature. Here, as so often, Chaucer breathes the breath of life into a formula already existing. As before animals are charmingly characterized,

> The kok, that orloge is of thorpes lyte;

he even makes the birds take after humans by dividing into social classes, fowls of ravine (the highest), and fowl who live on seeds, and on worms, and lowest of all the waterfowl. Critical good sense has seen this novelty as reflecting the social consciousness which appeared strikingly in the later fourteenth century, but it will hardly do to be so precise as to argue for a date just at the time of the Peasants' Revolt in 1381. Better evidence for date is Venus the planet seen north-north-west, which comes as near fitting 1382 as is needful, the best indication of date which we find. But we cannot fail to see awareness of patrician fastidiousness and delicacy in love at the courtship of the tercel and the formel eagle; as well as bourgeois impatience with them on the part of lesser fowl,

> Whan shal youre cursede pletynge have an ende?

The goose, says the poet ironically, "with here facounde gent," would settle the eagles' rivalry unideally,

> But she wol love hym, lat hym love another!

The gentler turtle-dove rebukes them—"if *you* wish a wight to speak, he would do well to be silent." The essence is the conflict between patrician contempt for vulgarity,

> The laughter aros of gentil foules alle,

and

> "Out of the donghil cam that word ful right,"

together with the sentiment of refined seed-fowl,

> "Nay, God forbede a lovere shulde chaunge!"
> The turtle seyde, and wex for shame al red,

over against the skepticism of actuality,

> "Wel bourded," quod the doke, "by myn hat!
> .   .   .   .   .
> There been mo sterres, God wot, than a peyre!"

Chaucer was not without some fellow-feeling for the second, as well as for the other.

Turning animals into individual people with the traits for which these animals are notorious did not start with Chaucer, nor even with the immortal *Roman de Renard,* from which he took the tale of Chantecleer and Pertelote in the *Nun's Priest's Tale;* so it made the *Parliament* not too startling. After this debate, Nature leaves to the beautiful formel eagle herself the choice between the tercel and his two rivals, and she with modest virginal caution begs with success to postpone her decision for a year. The other birds make their choices, which they ratify by embraces with wings and necks, and end with singing an exquisite rondeau, and they make such a shouting as they fly away that the sleeper awakes. The *Parliament* steadily increases its interest and vivacity, and ends in a climax, yet with a mild suspense; not too strong, for who can doubt that the formel in a year's time will choose the peerless tercel? The poem to any reader is clear, satisfying, and complete on the face of it.

The chief debate about the *Parliament* among scholars has been whether there is personal allegory in the formel and her three suitors. The guess that they represent actual per-

sons may well come to mind when one considers the appear-
ance of members of the royal family in the *Book of the
Duchess* and the prologue of the *Legend of Good Women*.
The application which has found most favor and for the
longest time is to the marriage of King Richard II (as the
tercel) and Anne of Bohemia (as the formel), which was
first considered in 1381 and took place in 1382. It would be a
satisfaction to close scholarship to settle on the date 1381-1382
for the *Parliament,* but this cannot be done. Not two but
three princes have been found who might correspond to the
two rivals of the noble tercel, but not suitors simultaneously
nor with certainty. It has also been remarked that it would
not be flattering to Chaucer's sovereign to show him as wait-
ing a year for a lady to decide between him and another, of
lower rank at that. There is little force in the suitors in the
poem and in history numbering three; three competitors or
what not are the usual number in story, from the Three
Bears back and forward. All one can say of this interpretation
is that some of these people might have casually strayed into
Chaucer's mind as he wrote, but that there is no proving it.
This identification is not the only one which has been offered,
there have been half-a-dozen others, some of them plausible
enough. When there is nothing otherwise unaccountable in a
narrative, it may be tempting to accept a single allegorical
interpretation; but the moment a plausible competing explanation appears, none can be taken seriously. If the inconc-
clusive ending may seem to some to point at the inconclu-
siveness of a situation in real life, one may ask if the slight
suspense of the actual ending is not less flat and obvious
than the alternative as an ending. We have the word of the
present poet-laureate of England that Chaucer's *Parliament
of Fowls* was what determined his dedication to poetry, and
one may well feel the poem sufficiently accounted for by the
varied richness of its course from the grandeur of the opening
to the beauty of love's garden, the amusing humanity of the
debate, the charm of the lyric ending.

CHAPTER SEVEN

THE LEGEND OF GOOD WOMEN

STILL compliant with fashionable literary custom, Chaucer in the *Legend of Good Women* combines two conventions—the love-vision and the adaptation of church language to the religion of love. As to the former, here again in the prologue of the *Legend* we find the dream-setting, the spring scene in a lovely garden, the joy in it, the classic mythology, the personifications, the bookish undercurrent. All this is found in the earlier of the two forms of prologue, that now usually called Prologue F, which is obviously the one to show the poet's original intention. This prologue goes far beyond any of his other love-visions in happy emotion. The poet repeatedly recurs to his feeling for a special flower, the lowly little pink and white daisy which so beautifies English lawns. The recurring intensity of the feeling avowed again and again for nearly two hundred lines may be a little surprising. No wight loved hotter in his life; he runs to see her close at night; she is his mistress, guide and sovereign lady, as if his god on earth; his busy ghost thirsts to see this youthful flower, constrains him with fiery desire to kneel at her opening in the morning sun; without sleep, meat, or drink he will lean on his elbow all day to watch the little daisy. Charming as this is, it must contain something besides poetry, coming as it does from a middle-aged political diplomatist. It is allowable to guess that behind it lie personal and social and human relations and feeling. He gives us a warning near the beginning that he is following a fashion, is imitating predecessors—"ye lovers who know how to write poems of feeling, ye have done the best of it before me, I come gleaning after you and am glad of any goodly word ye have left, and if I chance to re-hearse your fresh songs, be forbearing to me." Sure enough this prologue in structure and often in wording is full of bor-rowings from Machault, Froissart, Deschamps, not to men-tion Boccaccio. His devotion to the daisy comes specially from Deschamps' *Lai de Franchise* (where the "Marguerite" repre-sents originally a lady so named)—a poem written in 1385, and communicated to Chaucer at latest in 1386. This gives us the earliest possible date for the *Legend,* a date confirmed by the little garden-lodge which he mentions and which points to his country-dwelling in Greenwich from 1385, and not to his previous residence on the city-wall. Other facts be-sides Chaucer's intensity of language prepare us to think he had a real lady in mind. He uses *she* for the flower nearly as often as *it,* and also about as often addresses the daisy as *ye,* the deferential plural instead of the more familiar *thou.* All this is not without significance for understanding the poem. Years ago the authoress of an elementary history of English literature opined that "Chaucer had the heart of a simple child," to which a reviewer countered that this did not sug-gest the man who wrote the *Wife of Bath's Prologue.* The ex-planation is not that Chaucer was over-simple but that here more is meant than meets the ear.

The fact is that the feeling expressed for the daisy is to be passed on to a woman. When the God of Love appears, he is accompanied by the queen Alcestis with adornment which

Made hire lyk a daysie for to sene.

This is the queen of Thessaly, wife of Admetus, who gave herself to death in her husband's stead. She is the Good Woman *par excellence;* her legend would probably have closed the poem had Chaucer completed it. His interest in her is the more notable because she is not in Ovid's *Meta-*

morphoses where he found most of the Good Women, and indeed one cannot be sure where he did get his knowledge of
her. But it may well be doubted if Alcestis is the only actual
woman in mind in the poem, for in her closing words she
clearly surrenders her honors to a living woman, Queen Anne,
saying,

> And whan this book ys maad, yive it the quene,
> On my byhalf, at Eltham or at Sheene.

Alcestis is to pay over her tribute to Queen Anne at one or
other of her palaces; the author when his whole poem is
completed is to present it to her. What would it mean to say
that Alcestis is the daisy and that both are Queen Anne?
The identification of course is undefinable. It is impossible to
say more than that the poet is passing on to the Queen the
beauty, sweetness, and goodness of the daisy, and of the Greek
lady. Any reader or auditor could understand the prologue
in no other way than this, as high and unmistakable tribute
to Queen Anne. This does not deny the poet's sincere enjoyment of spring and its flowers. The association of the daisy,
Alcestis, and Anne heightens the charm of all three. It should
be needless to say that Alcestis as Anne by no means shows
that Cupid (who is not her husband) is Richard; the two
matters are unconnected.

In Prologue G things have changed. It takes its nickname
from the single manuscript which contains it, while F is usually so named from the best of its twelve independent early
authorities. That this version is not the first but the revised
version there is abundance of evidence, of which the most
conclusive is that, while there are borrowings in both versions from the three French poets mentioned above, there are
far more in F, and therefore that just before writing F
Chaucer must have been reading them. If G is the earlier,
since he had also read them before writing that, then in writing F he added to his mosaic with almost inconceivable care
and ingenuity. The alterations are mostly in the early and
middle portions with certain passages near the end which

the poet remembered to cancel, forgetting however to make certain other cancellations really demanded by the principles he was following in revising. Notably, in F Alcestis is not named till the end (except once, clumsily, though perhaps for an intelligible reason), where the poet is surprised to learn who she is; in G this last is unchanged, though earlier she has been named four times by characters and twice by the narrator. Otherwise version G is the more closely and logically ordered; but in the view of most critics (not of all) this by no means compensates for the loss in spontaneity and warmth.

If G is less emotionally attractive than F, why did Chaucer so alter it? But one may well also ask whether the charm of F may not in part be due to a modern feeling of patronage, whether it may not be due to pleasure in thinking that one of the great men of the past had the "heart of a simple child" which we enjoy meeting but should not wish to have ourselves. Do we at times like to feel that we, the heirs of all the ages, are superior without effort? Since the enthusiasm of F is unparalleled in Chaucer's poetry, he may have tempered it because of altered conditions and self-conscious feeling. The diplomatist in early middle age not too disillusioned but facing things as they are, after some years may have felt incongruity in leaning on his elbow all day long to contemplate the little pink daisy. This charms us, but also amuses us, and in Chaucer's day to surrender thus to a temporary fashion would also be amusing, perhaps too amusing. But the most illuminating change is the disappearance of the Queen; Alcestis no longer ends by directing the poem to her at Eltham or Sheene. This disappearance and that of so much of the intense feeling which seems so human it is hard not to associate together; the humanized flower and the living woman point to the same person. Since Queen Anne died in June of 1394 it seems almost certain that it was after that date that she was revised out of the prologue. But why the tribute to the Queen should have been removed one cannot see, unless the Queen's husband King Richard II was at the bottom of it, a highly neurotic man, emotionally very dependent on her, who after her death among other signs of feeling ordered the house at Sheene where she died torn down, though a favorite residence. We are justified in guessing the date of version G as late 1394, as that of version F to be 1385-1386.

The fact is that Chaucer was a sufficiently masculine man who lived in a mentally feminized society, and accepted the handicap of allowing himself to be much dominated by social ambition, the desire to please attractive people. His age was a backwater age in England, with no big, strongly growing motives to sweep through and scour out a channel, certainly none to draw him much. A man who wished to please was in danger of surrendering his best self, and thus Chaucer did in the *Legend*. That it did please his day is shown by the rather large number of manuscripts. The courtier accepted the behest of a young-girl queen with an effeminate husband, and affected transports over a sweet little flower, which afterwards in a belated maturing he was to acknowledge tacitly as a trifle silly.

The feeling and the nature-appeal of the prologue to the *Legend* undoubtedly comes from the love-vision heritage, but to some moderns there is nearly as much charm in its line of literary custom of long descent which adapts church language to the religion of love. The beauty of holiness adds more beauty to love, none the less for also making the more secular-minded moderns smile a little. The woman who is good in the religion of love flouts the Christian virtue of chastity; herein is the chief artificiality. Chaucer it appears has sinned against the religion of Love in writing of Criseyde and translating the *Roman de la Rose,* a heresy against Love's law, and near the end of the prologue Alcestis commands him to do penance by "making a glorious legend of good women that were true in loving all their lives." It is no less a work of piety to write what will glorify one of Cupid's saints and martyrs than what will glorify one of God's, to be read—

legenda—on his festival. Substantially the same title, "The Saints' Legend of Cupid," is given the poem when it is referred to in the *Man of Law's Prologue*. The rubric at the beginning and end of each of Chaucer's legends, as "Incipit legenda Cleopatriae, Martiris Egipti regine," follows the usage of Christian saints' legends, though not elsewhere, as in this instance, making readers of Shakespeare smile. Analogy to Christian tradition is unmistakable in the prologue. Cupid's mother Venus is "Seynt Venus," and ballades are "hymns for his holy days;" the daisy is his "relyke, digne and delytable." ("Relic" became extended to anything devoid of consciousness but with sacred associations; in the *Troilus* the palladium is called a Trojan relic.) Cupid's austerity is like that of Jesus Christ in many a popular tale, while Alcestis' charitable intercession succeeds like the Blessed Virgin's; a modern popular saying has it that Jesus represents the justice of God, and Mary his mercy. Anyone who has seen the Christus Pantocrator of mosaic in the semidome in the apse of great Lombard romanesque churches will recognize how it enforces austere awfulness. The prologue begins with a Catholic sort of argument—that we must credit what we read in books because we have no other evidence for what is so certain as the joy of heaven and the pain of hell; a passage which goes far to establish Chaucer's solidity in the religion of his time.

More epochal in literary history than anything else in the *Legend* is the verse. Chaucer's awareness of his innovation is shown when at the end of the earlier prologue Cupid charges him,

> Make the metres of hem as the lest.

Aside from the very fine ballade in the prologue (simpler in form than is usual with Chaucer) the whole poem is in the ten-syllable couplet, one of the greatest forms of verse in English poetry for flexibility, variety, dignity, distinction. It is not known to have been used before in English, unless by Chaucer himself in the *Palamon and Arcite*, which is named in this prologue and is probably substantially identical with the first of the *Canterbury Tales,* the *Knight's,* which is in that verse but which may not have been completed when here mentioned. Outside Chaucer it is unknown earlier in English, and is rare anywhere else. Its usefulness and versatility in Chaucer is shown all the way from the *Miller's Tale* and the *Wife's Prologue* to the *Franklin's* and the *Pardoner's Tales.* But there is even more than this. If Chaucer introduced the couplet of Keats, he also introduced that of Pope, the unified, closed, high-polished couplet full of balance and antithesis, and what is more he shows us what is its origin. Where could we find a better specimen (out of many others in Chaucer) than at the end of the legend of Medea in her words to Jason?

> Whi lykede me thy yelwe her to se
> More than the boundes of myn honeste?
> Why lykede me thy youthe and thy fayrnesse,
> And of thy tonge the infynyt graciousnesse?
> O, haddest thow in thy conquest ded ybe,
> Ful mikel untrouthe hadde ther deyd with the!

This comes straight (though heightened) from Ovid's *Heroides,* xii,

> Cur umquam Colchi Magnetida vidimus Argon,
>   turbaque Phasiacam Graia bibistis aquam?
> Cur mihi plus aequo flavi placuere capilli
>   et decor et linguae gratia ficta tuae?
> . . . . .
> Quantum perfidiae tecum, scelerate, perisset,
>   dempta forent capiti quam mala multa meo!

Such stylized lines as Medea's are frequent in the *Legend,* both when found in the Latin and when not, stimulated by the echoing of Ovid. In essence these are the neo-classic closed couplets of the English seventeenth and eighteenth century, and without being a constant mannerism of Chaucer they often recur among his ten-syllable couplets. They are congenial to one of his aspects, his rational, realistic, satiric side that has so appealed to the neo-classic English of two centuries ago, and to moderns sympathetic with the eighteenth century. This poetic aspect illustrates the wide scope of the poet who ranges from the *Reeve's Tale* to the *Prioress's* and to *Truth*. What is just as interesting, this shows where the later English neo-classic couplet came from—the Latin elegiac distich. Though the latter is not of two identical lines, but of a hexameter and a pentameter, not only is it one of the most magnificent and agreeable forms of verse, but except for the unidentical structure of the lines it has all the other mannerisms of the English neo-classic couplet. This as the origin of the couplet is established by the latter's increasing recurrence in English poetry of the eighteenth and following centuries, at first in translations and imitations of Ovid's elegiac distichs, before becoming visibly cultivated in independent and original narrative and reflective poetry. This has been fully established by a living scholar, in a work unfortunately not fully in print.[1]

There is much in the legends proper that does not dispose us to believe the collection a spontaneous product of Chaucer's imagination. The stock criticism of their contents is of their monotony and uniformity—lovely women star-crossed in love, a subject of which a masculine man like Chaucer, not really sentimental, would be bound to weary. That he repeatedly shows weariness was pointed out many years ago; he shows this throughout in a dozen or two passages: Love in the prologue bids him write briefly; he says little of the reception of Demophoön by Phyllis because he is sick of his subject, and must hasten him in his *Legend*, which he prays God to help him finish; he will rehearse but a word or two of her letter, for he will not vouchsafe "to swink on" Demophoön, "nor spend on him a pen full of ink." His heart is not

---

[1] For the relation here mentioned by Dr. Tatlock between the heroic couplet and the Latin elegiac distich, see Tatlock (*Nation*, XCVIII, Apr. 9, 1914, 390), E. C. Knowlton (*Nation*, XCIX, July 30, 1941, 134), A. M. Clark (*The Library*, 4th Ser., III, no. 3, Dec., 1922, 210-22), G. P. Shannon (*PMLA*, XLV, June, 1930, 532-42), and R. C. Wallerstein (*PMLA*, L, March, 1935, 166-209).

in his picture-gallery of emotional betrayed damsels. The directing or giving of the *Legend* to Queen Anne has suggested to many critics that it was written at the request of the Queen, as is stated in so many words by the poet's disciple and younger contemporary John Lydgate, who is most unlikely not to have been well informed about him, and indeed probably knew him personally. The prologue of the *Legend* even intimates that Chaucer may have been bidden to write the *Troilus* and the *Rose* by someone whom he could not flout; with his connections with the great this may well often have happened. That Chaucer had the happy young queen in mind, he shows in postponing the *Good* Women ill-used by traitor-men, and beginning with a queen and another woman (Cleopatra and Thisbe) happy in their love, whose only enemy is Fate. This evades the tactlessness of at the first ignoring Anne's congenial marriage.

With the usual canonizing of classical literature, none of the legends is from recent or scriptural history; all ten are from the classics, and so are nearly all the women listed in the balade in the prologue, and in the Man of Law's list, which Chaucer evidently held as a storage of ladies for possible continuation. The very names of Cleopatra, Thisbe, Dido, Hypsipyle, Medea, Lucretia, Ariadne, Philomela, Phyllis, Hypermnestra show that what lies behind the *Legend* is literary tradition, beauty (not to say sometimes prettiness), rather than as in the *Troilus* the quickening of living contemporary imagination into far more living imagination and observation of Chaucer's own. The lyric element, the pretense that the betrayed ladies are addressing or writing to their men, comes from Ovid's *Heroides,* a group of his most skilful though artificial poems where women do just this. In using these, Chaucer was helped by a fourteenth-century Italian prose translation ascribed to one Ceffi (as so often elsewhere he makes some use of vernacular versions of Latin); this may account for his frequent use of Italian forms of Latin proper names. Some of the matter comes from Ovid's

Metamorphoses, the *Aeneid,* other classics, and from medieval encyclopedic works and other retelling of ancient narrative, without discrimination between history and tradition. Many of the legends show evidence of somewhat wide reading, and justify their author's reputation for centuries as "our learned Chaucer." Though the style in the *Legend* has Chaucer's inevitable finish and charm, it seldom has a magical touch, and further he rarely means to make us smile as he would, had his arm felt quite free. He cannot quite refrain from this latter: he prays God let our heads never ache ere he finds a man as true as Anthony; of Jason the seducer, he observes

> Ever as tendre a capoun et the fox,
>
> . . . . .
> As shal the good-man that therfore hath payed;

after the legend of Phyllis, he says

> And trusteth, as in love, no man but me.

But the subject of the legends inevitably encourages Chaucer's softer, pitiful side though sometimes expressed vigorously:

> Have at thee, Jason! Now thyn horn is blowe!

So does the polite French background with its feminism. He cuts out the worst horror of the Philomela story, the cannibalism, just as the Man of Law rejects the incest of Canacee and Antiochus. When Chaucer reaches his announced subject he surrenders to Ovid, the spokesman of an age not unlike his own, when ambitious politicians were willing to accept the countenance of skilful literary men, whose attraction to women would make pleasant intervening lunchtable chat. The legends therefore are soft, redolent of pity for the human beings who have lost out in the perennial duel between male aggression and female defense. Chaucer of course accepts the assumption of chivalry—that if man is the stronger it is better for humanity that he should give way. But in his later manner, that of the *Canterbury Tales,* he

makes things lifelike: humanly, in the delightful account of
the sisters Ariadne and Phaedra, their talk and their romantic
interest in Theseus—an attractive young man doubles feminine tenderheartedness; externally, as in the graphic account
of Cleopatra's sea-fight, full of touches from sea-fights of his
own day, including cannon, and as in the grisly account of
her death, which may well reflect rumors from Egypt in his
own day.

The modern reader is likely to agree with what he fancies
was Chaucer's feeling about the uniformity of the legends,
especially in contrast with the extraordinary variety and con-
trasts of the *Canterbury Tales* in point, tendency, and style.
The only moderate growth in variety and originality during
the preceding ten years, in his thirties and forties, makes one
realize how much occupied he was in the surface-affairs of the
world, perhaps with insufficient leisure to spread his fields to
rain and sunshine for those to draw up the nutriment from
his own past and own powers. Growth of a poetic personality,
especially in the conservative Middle Ages, may be very
gradual.

CHAPTER EIGHT

LESS CONSPICUOUS WORKS

THE ORIGINAL of one of Chaucer's less important works, his prose translation of Boethius' *On the Consolation of Philosophy,* in itself is enormously important. One of the chief links between classical and medieval literature and thought, it had helped to win cultivated Latins to Christianity; down to the Renascence of the twelfth century, Boethius, heir of all the earlier ages, was the chief link to classical philosophy. An orthodox Christian, it is believed, and author of several theological tractates in favor of Catholic orthodoxy and against heresies, he is more important for having transmitted to the Latin West most of the Aristotle that the early Middle Ages possessed. An intellectually brilliant member of a prominent Roman family, he had been employed by the government of the Ostrogoth Theodoric, but was suspected by it of disloyalty, unjustly he avers, and put to death in early middle age in 524. While in prison, he wrote the *Consolation,* still highly appealing for the originality and learning of its bracing courage and the originality and beauty of its imaginative style. Its immense influence for many centuries is due to its presenting some of the cream of ancient philosophy in such a way as to harmonize with the Christianity which explicitly it ignores and as to show cultivated people that the two systems at bottom teach much that is the same about the nature of God and of good, about how to bear the assaults of Fortune with the help of reason, about free-will and destiny, the relation of reward and punishment to desert. The Christian Boethius' perception in supporting the Christian feeling about such things without introducing Christian language was rewarded by the immensity of his vogue among the cultivated for twelve centuries, as late as in Anatole France's *Rôtisserie de la Reine Pédauque,* and by the fact that in English the book was translated by two of the greatest sovereigns (Alfred and Elizabeth) and one of the greatest poets, an unparalleled tribute. The fact that a modern reads the book largely with a sense of its pathos makes him feel how enormously our attitude about such matters has become confused.

With Chaucer's usual and perhaps fitting modesty about his prowess in Latin, he made constant use beside the Latin of a thirteenth-century French version attributed to Jean de Meun and a Latin commentary of the next century by Nicholas Trivet. Because of his efforts to reproduce the meaning exactly (as he does fairly well) his version is both wordy and clumsy, seldom easy or felicitous like his verse. This care, as well as the existence of the translation at all, is due to Chaucer's deep admiration for Boethius, to whom he owed much of his knowledge of ancient thought, and whom he often names and far oftener quotes. The specially abundant use of the *Consolation* in the *Troilus* justifies the supposition that the translation was made not far from the date of that poem, and the charming and highly characteristic stanza called *Words unto Adam* about the same time since his scribe appears therein as making copies of "Boece or Troylus."

A number of the minor poems, most of them quite likely from late in Chaucer's life, owe special debt to the *Consolation.* One of the longest is that called usually *The Former Age,* based on the fifth poem in Boethius' second book, and describing one of the classical ideas of the simple life projected back into the beginnings of the human race: subsistence on the natural fruits of the earth, without agriculture or milling or cookery or wine; no dyeing, no building, no commerce, no mining, no luxury, conquest, or warfare. The picture is more attractive, especially to the imaginatively in-dolent, than the Garden of Eden, where man must till the soil. Hebrew literature throughout had the ethical spirit of the prophets. The classical ancients, while they also had a more strenuous picture of the golden age, could surrender their ethics and their good sense for a while to an existence of lolling; even so strenuous an idealist as Boethius could sur-render to its combination with peaceableness; it would appeal as much at moments to Christians who accepted the orthodox unstrenuous idea of heaven. The other Boethian poems, *Fortune, Truth, Gentilesse, Lack of Steadfastness,* have been to some readers the most attractive of Chaucer's lyrics. Cool ethical poems fit the characteristic mood of the nineteenth rather than of the mid-twentieth century, and carry our thoughts to Matthew Arnold and Clough, to Longfellow and other American poets in the Puritan tradition. But since ethics are at the base of the conduct of life, the poet who can express it beautifully and memorably deserves well of us; even if such a feeling may seem priggish to some, no one will call Chaucer priggish. Though he was following a temporary French taste, perhaps not always deeply felt, in Deschamps and others, Chaucer's sincerity is manifest, especially in *For-tune* and *Truth* with their virtues of courage and good sense. In form the four poems are *ballades,* of three stanzas with repetition of rime and a repeated refrain; some of them con-clude with an *envoi* containing a practical application or ad-dress. A *ballade* was in origin a dance-poem, to be sung, the air and above all the marked rhythm being originally the es-sential to carry the dance.

The half-dozen other ballades are on various subjects, a few, as commonly, being personal love-poems. These are not neces-sarily on serious love, especially the light and delicious *To Rosemounde;* indeed we know nothing at all about Chaucer's emotional life, except for reason to suspect that his marriage was not of the most successful. Similar to ballades are the two late Envoys to personal friends, Scogan and Bukton. The second rather advises against marriage, out of Chaucer's own experience; the first, less serious, by reproaching Scogan for inconstancy in love, then more seriously voicing the occasional pessimism of a man beginning to feel his years and the decay of his powers, and feeling forgotten by the great world. Of all Chaucer's poems it is the most pathetic. Both men have been identified as of Chaucer's circle, though there is ambiguity in the case of Bukton. The *Complaint to his Purse,* a ballade, follows with cleverness the custom, in days when poets had no professional means of support except through patrons, of appeal to them, in this case to King Henry IV, who acceded in 1399. The Envoy to him at the end of it is the latest production which can be dated. Chaucer's purse is his lady, and of course he would not have his lady "light."

A number of his poems beside the one just mentioned are called Complaints, a vague word variously used for lament and even fault-finding, but often for an expression of thwarted love or the like, which may be highly lyrical. Chaucer's genius is not greatly lyrical, and these poems mostly have little feeling; but some of them experiment in technique, the *Complaint to his Lady* containing the first specimen in English of Dante's *terza rima,* and some being in ballade form.

The Complaint of Mars is highly characteristic of Chaucer, in celebrating St. Valentine's Day (like the *Parliament of Fowls,* through the speech of birds), and even more, in its interest in astrology. The *amour* of Mars and Venus is from the fourth book of Ovid's *Metamorphoses;* the originality of the poem lies in appropriating it to an astrological situation, a conjunction of the two planets described in technical detail. This points to no precise date; the twelfth of April in line 139 seems unexplained. Even in the fifteenth century the poem was taken as symbolical of a scandal at court, but this is highly doubtful. While it looks *a priori* likely enough, Chaucer's interest in astrology may have been enough to stimulate his imagination into "making." But critics probably have not yet said the last word. The *Complaint of Venus* owes its title, apparently supplied by some fifteenth-century scribe, to the probably groundless supposition that it is a pendant to that of Mars, and that both allude to this notorious *amour* at court, but there is no reference to Venus in the poem. Adapted as three ballades from ballades by Otes de Granson, a French poet at Richard's court who died in 1397, its most interesting part is the highly original and pathetic envoy, showing some of the pessimism of declining years. Age appears elsewhere too; a line with one foot too many (line 81) is common in the writing of the aging Chaucer (as well as of the inexperienced) ; the poet also notes the scarcity of rhymes in English. This is one of Chaucer's poems, like the *House of Fame,* where he unconventionally speaks out about himself. But it also shows how till near the end he cared about maintaining his relations with the fashionable, though without surrender.

Naturally there are some short poems which may be by Chaucer and may not. Among his papers after his death would be found odd loose papers or waxed tablets written by him or others which at the time he valued. Who could then, or now, be sure whether he was the author? Even if whoever took responsibility after his death chose to "release" them with a statement "by Chaucer," we now are not justified in positively accepting them without other evidence; still less if they have no such statement. But if they follow his usages as to versification and as to language at a time when the latter was rapidly changing, and if they "sound like Chaucer" in the ear of a modern critic saturated with his poetry, it is safest tentatively to accept them. On these grounds, one may thus accept, among the five so classified by Mr. Robinson, the first, *Against Women Unconstant,* and above all the third. For the genuineness of *Merciles Beaute* (identical in form with the rondeau which ends the *Parliament of Fowls)* some moderns would almost go to the stake.

These less prominent poems are fairly representative of Chaucer on various sides, conventional, gay, serious, though less on his inventive and imaginative side. They have his variety and originality, his good sense and above all his vitality, which have kept him alive to the present day. Even in that unharmonious seventeenth century Lady Anne Clifford, cultivated but not educated, in her older and saddened years, could write that she was "comforted by the excellent Chaucer's book,"—"I were in a pitiable case, having as many troubles as I have, but when I read in that, I scorn and make light of them all, and a little part of his beauteous spirit infuses itself in me."

CHAPTER NINE

The Canterbury Tales

THE *Legend of Good Women,* with its highly personal prologue containing Chaucer as one of the personages, followed by the somewhat varied legends, evidently stimulated a wish to do something of the same general sort but more ambitious and varied. Hence the *Canterbury Tales.* That he still contemplated the possibility of continuing the legends, perhaps because some one he did not wish to disappoint expected this of him, one can see from his mention in the *Man of Law's Prologue* of legends presumably never written. But it is not surprising that he seems never to have done so, in view of the vast and attractive prospect for the road to Canterbury and back to Southwark and the doings at both places. The plan allowed the writing of several kinds of narrative he had never yet essayed, which freed his spirit from bondage to the Roman and the French past; no one can fail to detect the author's enjoyment in the tales of real life.

The charm, and the vital and dramatic and *thick* character of the frame-story, narratives told by personages in a containing narrative, is found in a good many earlier works known to Chaucer in several languages from Ovid's *Metamorphoses* down. There is no reason to fancy that Chaucer got the idea of this particular frame of a pilgrimage from one he had himself taken (though, as an at least ordinarily religious man, he had probably taken many, and story-telling is known to have been a common diversion on such journeys). He may well have almost daily seen pilgrims to St. Thomas' shrine in Canterbury, one of the most popular and easily reached in England, for there is ground for believing that, for years after 1385, he lived in Greenwich. Further, the shortest sea route from London to the Continent took travelers through Canterbury on the way to Dover. Chaucer no doubt had followed that road a number of times.

As to antecedents in literature, no earlier account of story-telling on a journey exists that is at all likely to have suggested the Canterbury pilgrimage. This refers especially to what at first may seem a rather striking parallel, the *Novelle* of Giovanni Sercambi, a man of high standing in the Italian city of Lucca. The book is a rather dull and poor imitation of Boccaccio's *Decameron*. To shun their plague-infested town a large and varied assortment of Luccanese travel pretty much all over Italy mostly afoot, and among their pastimes in the narrative are tales which are all told by Sercambi himself. Two versions are known. Of that supposed to have been written in 1374, only one copy is known to have existed, and that is now lost. The later form, not finished before 1386, exists in only one manuscript. Though the outline of story-telling, if not on a pilgrimage at any rate on a journey, resembles the *Canterbury Tales* more than does any other earlier work, and in point of date might have become known to Chaucer on his second visit to Italy, and even by hearsay on his first slightly before its probable date of completion, nevertheless, to speak broadly and without illusion, the chances are much against this. The chief consideration is not the poorness of the composition but the small number of copies known of the work and the consequent lack of evidence for familiarity with it. In the illiterate Middle Ages, where two or three were gathered together public story-telling was all but universal.

If it is worth while to suggest any specific model (which may be questioned), it is best to name him to whom Chau-

cer always owed most in congeniality and in matter, Boccaccio.
I do not enlarge on the "Questioni d'Amore" episode in his
Filocolo, a clear case of frame-story embedded in a longer
work which Chaucer very probably knew; one of the tales
in the frame is believed to be the origin of the *Franklin's
Tale.* Nor do I enlarge on the less similar framed narrative
in Boccaccio's *Ameto.* It has long been usual to reject any
knowledge by Chaucer of the *Decameron,* chiefly on the
ground that, had he known it, this should be unmistakable
through borrowings; that the work is without certain marked
elements of Chaucer's poem, the variety of the people, and
the tales told during the journey, makes influence at least
unconvincing. This is valid argument. On the other hand,
there are certain considerations to the opposite effect. To say
the least, Chaucer was more congenially indebted to no other
writer than to Boccaccio. The matter of his two longest
poems, the *Troilus* and the *Knight's Tale,* besides considerable passages in some others, came from Boccaccio's *Filostrato*
and *Teseide;* and the *Troilus* and the *Franklin's Tale* are believed to be heavily indebted to the *Filocolo;* we should also
mention his familiarity with Boccaccio's Latin works. In view
of his several months of sojourn and travel in Italy, including
a visit to Florence, and in view of his taste for reading and
inexhaustible curiosity, it is incredible that he had not heard
of the *Decameron,* and indeed seen it. If he never bought a
copy, that may have been because it was a very large and
expensive book and he was not an affluent man. No one can
doubt that it would have appealed to him, with its variety,
beauty, and ideality, to say nothing of its inexhaustible en-
tertainingness. Like many of the long and great books, the
Decameron should be read leisurely; it will produce not chiefly grins and snickers, but something of the feeling of the *Ode
to a Grecian Urn,* youthful passionate beauty caught and
perpetuated:

Cold Pastoral!
When old age shall this generation waste,
Thou shalt remain.

To read the *Decameron* all through slowly and quietly is a genuine experience. As to proof of Chaucer's knowledge of it, undeniable direct borrowings there are none; but there are passages so similar as to suggest reminiscence, and both works contain some four times a similar or identical story, but in most cases the story is known elsewhere in a form more like Chaucer's. The four cases are the tales of the Clerk, the Merchant, the Franklin and the Shipman (one may disregard the Man of Law's, as much remoter from V,2 in the *Decameron*). The *Clerk's Tale* is derived from the last story in the *Decameron*, indirectly, through the Latin version of Petrarch. In the other three cases, an acceptable explanation of the resemblances to Boccaccio is that, having read his book in Italy, Chaucer remembered certain of its contents, and later came across other versions. In one case, the *Shipman's Tale*, Chaucer may have used no other version than that in the *Decameron*, VIII,1. Whether or not these likenesses in contents are further evidence for his knowledge of it, some find it hard to doubt this knowledge, and if it were needful to pick out a single original for the *Tales* (as it is not) there is none more plausible than the *Decameron*, assuredly none more attractive.

Beside the fact that the *Legend of Good Women* is a kind of frame-story, an essential sign of its influence is in the verse of most of the *Tales*, the ten-syllable couplet. An especially unmistakable type of it is the closed and balanced couplet, the effectiveness of which Chaucer seems to have learned from Ovid. It appears in a dozen striking cases in the general *Prologue*:

> Nowher so bisy a man as he ther nas,
> And yet he semed bisier than he was.

It may be doubted if this device of style was ever in the forefront of his consciousness, as it was with Dryden and especially Pope, but it was always ready to slip responsively into gear—one reason why modern Chaucerians feel at home in the eighteenth century, and why that time felt at home with

him. We shall see later why this device reappears from time
to time in his poems.

The Prologue

The earth on which in Chaucer's poetry we have been living and moving hitherto is much like the background of
Botticelli's paintings, improved and park-like nature, not like
the usual actual earth, which seemed to the medievals dan-
gerous and uncomfortable. Wild nature was full of beasts
and bandits and thorns; grand scenery hardly appeared in
literature outside Milton's hell till the intensifying of civilization in the eighteenth century, and the widespread enjoyment of it today owes much to Pullman-cars, luxurious steam-
ers, and automobiles. Workaday nature had little appeal to
taste before the day of sentimentalism and democracy. But
it is this which opens the *Canterbury Tales,* and which prepares us to merge ancient Athens with Trumpington, Arthur's court with "a marshy country called Holderness." So
the *Prologue* begins with light April showers following blus-
tery March, with the budding leaves in holts and heaths, and
with singing breeding birds. This is neither wild nor park-
like nature, but workaday actual England, the only fitting
background for the people in the *Prologue.*

The people in the *Prologue* make us realize that we are
near the beginnings of modern literature, for in general they
are middle-class; none outranks the Knight, or the Monk
(who ranks as a prior), none is beneath the rather prosper-
ous Plowman. The persons might appear as mere names; or
as vague types; or as vivid types; or as individuals. As befits
poetry, which deals with general truth, vivid types are what
decidedly they are, though sometimes with individual and
non-typical traits (as with the Cook and the Wife of Bath).
The spirit is rationalistic; Chaucer is becoming fully his
essential self, realistic, not romantic, which he actually is
only superficially and at times. Accordingly the descriptions
tend to be short and condensed, and also to be epigrammatic.

That is why the ten-syllable couplet is fitting, and each element of form aids the other; and why the Ovidian closed and balanced couplet tends to recur. When we come to the separate tales, we shall glance at the descriptions of the tellers, to which there are allusions, and to which the tales are often though not always fitted, though the momentary emotional situation often dictates the character of a tale. Some of the pilgrims in this unfinished work tell no tales. One is the Yeoman, vivid, ideal, on the surface; others the Haberdasher and his four mates, all workers for trade (with a delicious reference to their socially ambitious wives), and the Plowman. The lifelike and genial ending of the *Prologue* announces the plan, two tales from each on the outward journey, and two on the return, to end with a supper at the Host's inn. Of this immense plan, only one-fifth is carried out; completed, it would have been the longest of English poems, and assuredly would have been a challenge to the poet to maintain his now unflagging vitality.

None of the people is more lifelike than the Host; used to dealing with most kinds of people, authoritative with the common sort, but too deferential with the superior (to whom an inn-keeper would be less used), by no means always delicately tactful, but emotionally responsive to the various tales, with his finger on the pulse of the company, but impulsively liable to lose his temper and even break the peace. He is a good toast-master and a crafty manager. *After* they have paid their bills, he proposes the program of entertainment; the company in holiday-mood instantly agree that he shall be their governor, any rebel shall pay all the expenses of the journey, and the prize for the best tale (decided on by him) shall be a supper on their return, in his inn "Heere in this place, sittynge by this post," as he claps his hand on it. What a fresh key-note after the *Legend of Good Women!* Next day there is a pretense of choosing the first tale-teller by drawing lots, but we cannot believe that for the first the Host depended on chance for securing the Knight, highest of the

laity, and certain to define a high and decorous level before
a very mixed group.

The Knight's Tale

In the *Legend of Good Women*, while she plays her Virgin-
Mary part of intercessor, Alcestis names various poems by
Chaucer favorable to women, among them,

> al the love of Palamon and Arcite
> Of Thebes, thogh the storye ys known lyte.

No one doubts that this is substantially the *Knight's Tale*,
perhaps then unfinished and presumably unpublished. There
is no reason to believe it much rewritten for the *Canterbury
Tales*, save for addition of the first paragraphs and the final
line; to rewrite would be contrary to busy Chaucer's practice,
and to all probability. That it fits the *Canterbury Tales* so
well suggests that he was getting into tune with the new
narrative manner, and perhaps had already planned the
Tales. Its almost sole source, save for many short reminiscences here and there, is a work which he had long known
and used, the *Teseide* of Boccaccio, in a very peculiar sense
his chief and congenial master. Perhaps Chaucer would not
have admitted this, was not even aware of it; but it is true.
This poem, the *Teseide*, he had borrowed from repeatedly before, and it was to be highly influential on Italian literature
for two centuries; Boccaccio's attractive modesty has tended
to blind modern critics to his extraordinary creative originality as well as immense activity, and his effect on Pulci, Boi-
ardo, Ariosto, and Tasso, and through them on such foreign-
ers as Spenser. The *Teseide* is duplex, attempting to combine
the epic stately manner of the ancient Romans, of Statius and
Virgil, with medieval romance. The former manner influenced Chaucer in his *Anelida* and *Troilus* and elsewhere, but
he later abandoned it, and the *Knight's Tale* takes over the
romantic narrative of the *Teseide,* and is pure romance,
though starting with a perfunctory epic quotation from
Statius and summary of Boccaccio's epic beginning. The rest

is a condensation of Boccaccio's romantic narrative. But none of his works is more thoroughly Chaucerian.

Boccaccio seldom means to be humorous except broadly and unmistakably so; he took scholarship and a learned background very seriously; his works, to speak generally, are either scholarship, or imaginative romance, or bluntly and somewhat crudely popular. Chaucer's was a more completely harmonious and unified personality, which when he grew more fully into himself showed itself so characteristically that we could scarcely ever hesitate as to his authorship of any of his longer works. Amusing touches, delicate ridicule (though what is felt as amusing varies much from generation to generation) abound throughout his works, and by one who knows him and his day are constantly and unmistakably to be found or at least suspected, and constantly add to the delightfulness of his in general more serious works. It is a grievous mistake not to see such touches even in the *Parson's Tale*. Chaucer's personality is one of the most marked and individual in literary history. What has been said is very true of the *Knight's Tale*. The Knight is roguish when he tells of Emily's ceremonial bathing—how she did her rite he dare not tell—yet it were a game to hear all. Venus, disappointed at not getting her way, lets fall her tears in the very lists. Enumerating what he is not going to tell us the poet gives a brisk account of all that happens, which of itself makes us smile. Duke Theseus, the most lifelike and human of the persons, is highly amused at the woodland combat of the two knights over a girl ignorant, he says, of their existence. When the woods are felled for Arcite's pyre, the sylvan gods run up and down (like field-mice) disinherited of their habitation; one smiles again at the brisk outline sketched by listing what we shall *not* be told. Finally no one can miss the satire on old Egeus' commonplace consolation—just as no one ever died without living, so no one lived without dying.

Beside the lightness just mentioned, there is speed; no English poet can vary his rate—or seeming rate—as Chaucer

can. He uses devices and illusions beside listing what he
does not mean to tell us—he leaves the noble duke riding to
Athens; shortly to tell is his intent. Before we know it we
have everything, as in other poems as well. This poem however is rather fluent than epigrammatic, without the balance
and closure that the *Legend* and later poems learned from
Ovid, and that hardly produces narrative brevity; it is marked
rather by variety and vitality. Yet the *Teseide,* with its leisurely stanzas is reduced to less than a quarter. The stanzas of
the *Troilus* had lengthened far beyond Chaucer's intention;
here he intended less reflection, feeling, and personalities
than picturesqueness and activity. The tale, however, is anything but a mere bald summary; variety is achieved chiefly
by handsome description, also by emotion. It is hard to think
of a better proportioned and more satisfying poem of its kind.

Being the first of the *Canterbury Tales* and one of the most
sharply medieval, the Knight's has been one of the most influential and, at least in the last century (less so in the eighteenth), has given the impression that Chaucer is more romantic than he is. The tale is highly decorative and full of
chivalry; the practical, serviceable Knight enjoys renewing
his youth. It is full of ideal romantic love, not of artificial
"courtly love." Yet with Chaucer's growing clean-cut perception of personality, the people here are sharper than in Boccaccio. While Emily in the latter carries more of the plot, and
in the *Knight's Tale* is merely someone to love and marry,
the two lovers are fully individual, Palamon sentimental,
less magnanimous and masculine, Arcite a fully attractive
young male preferring disappointment to dishonor. Yet the
account of his death, though touching, is detached; the poet
has not surrendered to his imagination but holds on to
reality. A keen reading shows a trace of ironic reality in the
reward going to the less worthy lover. Chaucer is now in the
Canterbury period, and is lighter, actual, not merely decorative and traditional. Egeus is an individual. So above all is
Theseus, the true hero from beginning to end, in contrast

with the two attractive boys, virile, humane and above all adult; lifelike, without self-importance or pomp. All the people are merely outlined, but with firmness. In regard to grasp and proportion in characterizing Chaucer is fully mature. Brilliant description, clean-cut outlines of people, light romantic feeling, the *Knight's Tale* has confirmed the modern conception of the Middle Ages; with the personality of Theseus behind to steady it.

The Miller's Tale

The *Knight's Tale* has done what the Host wished, is called "a noble storie" by "the gentils everichon"; the Host drops the pretense of drawing lots, and in order to continue the high level calls on the highest of the clergy, the Monk. But the Miller, who is pale with too much to drink already—he knows he is drunk by the sound of his voice, he deliciously says—thinks otherwise, wishes to give the rest what he thinks fun. The impulsive Host, from being tactfully soothing, then less tactfully bidding him defer to some socially better man, bursts out that he is a fool. The host always tries to keep the peace, but is decidedly a respecter of persons and bullies the lower sort sometime till the peace is well broken. Then comes the dispute with the Reeve, who is sober, the first of the fallings-out that bring so much of the vitality of the whole work. Drunk as he is, the Miller expresses some wisdom, followed by Chaucer's apology for the churl's tale—turn over the page and choose another, there is enough historical matter to please patricians, and morality, and religion—a fair description of the whole set of narratives. The drama of the *Tales* is fully under way.

With the Miller's story, Chaucer enters a rich field utterly fresh to him; brilliant reality of the surface. Of fabliaux, commonly so-called, there are a half-dozen or more among the tales. The fabliau especially flourished in medieval French, and later in Italian, not much in English outside Chaucer. For the most part it is almost unmixed narrative, plot the main thing, full of dramatic irony and poetic justice; its purpose is sheer amusement, and it will stick at nothing, not at the fantastic, or even the impossible, assuredly not at the coarse and the obscene, the crude, and the cruel. Narratives of this sort abound in Boccaccio's *Decameron,* and if Chaucer had seen it, that may have disposed him to include some such tales. Chaucer's fabliaux however were enriched also with brilliant description and sharp characterization, really their chief attraction. Their element of reality makes them timeless, even contemporary, in contrast with the more ideal *Tales,* for ideals change from age to age, while reality essentially does not.

No direct source is known for the *Miller's Tale,* but there are so many close analogues that it unquestionably had a source, probably in French, and possibly known to Chaucer not in writing but through hearsay. He never wrote more brilliantly, but happily the brilliance is not artificial nor overdone. The poem is full of touches of reality which no medieval but Chaucer would have thought of—a hole in the door where the cat was wont to creep in, the carpenter snoring because sleeping in a cramped posture. It is full of lines, and of words, which light up the page, and since the aim is merely superficial effect the Ovidian closed and balanced couplet is not inappropriate. Here occurs, in describing Alison the wife, the couplet which Dryden extracts to show (which makes the modern smile a little) that Chaucer had some of the seventeenth-century skill in verse,

> Wynsynge she was as is a joly colt,
> Long as a mast, and upright as a bolt.

It so chances that this passes without jerks into modern English, and thus struck Dryden, who was ignorant of the history of English pronunciation. According to the paradox of imaginative literature while the coarseness of the incident fits the Miller's personality, the skill of the planning and the brilliance of the descriptions and skill of the style show the poet at his best; no poet will sacrifice excellence to fit an unworthy speaker, nor will pull down what might be to the level of what would be. Out of the mouths of churls come wisdom and beauty. The exaltation of style maintains the artificial ideality of the supposedly spontaneous tales being in verse, which ordinary humans do not talk in. The young men are essentially undiscriminated, both incautious and therefore finally foiled, but the humane Chaucer cannot but make the good-hearted John the carpenter, whose first thought in danger is for his young wife, just a trifle pathetic. The fabliaux show Chaucer's individuality very acutely.

The Reeve's Tale

The elderly Reeve, manager of an estate for some careless young patrician, is one of the most vividly though not sensationally described of the pilgrims in the *Prologue*—competent, crafty, suspicious and *tight* in physique and personality. A carpenter by calling, he resents the coarse Miller's shabby picture of another carpenter's plight, and exposes another miller in a tale which otherwise would seem out of character. In his own prologue, he tends to the moralizing loquacity of his years and like other of the humbler folk is ridiculed by the Host for it; we forgive the Reeve because of the beautiful appropriateness of his language to his rustic life. The Host would hurry him, they are passing Greenwich, "ther many a shrewe is inne," says the poet no doubt chaffing the town where he was then living. The most interesting thing in this prologue, as well as in the tale, is the use of the northern dialect (*ik* for *I, gas* for *goeth, til* for *to*). Chaucer, unlike unskilful moderns, knew that a dialect-story should give only a flavor and hint, not a tiresome phonetic record of the speech. Chaucer and George Birmingham's Irish stories are the best at this.

The *Reeve's Tale* is almost more brilliant than the *Miller's,* with its constant reversals of fortune, its poetic justice, its bitter sarcasm, its balanced Ovidian couplets; the characterization, even keener than in the preceding Tale. The miller is a bluffer and a bully, but shrewd and penetrating, and full

of the cheap chaffing with which the uneducated still bore
university men; his wife, arrogant and touchy because a bas-
tard; their daughter, looking like her father with an added
trait, the sentimentality of the sensual. They are a pretty
family. The very horse of the clerks, making off to the fen
to chase wild mares, is as much preoccupied with sex as his
masters. Though these two are little distinguished, Alan is
more enterprising, and gives some hint that he had earlier
cast a desirous eye on the daughter. There can be no doubt
that this tale too is from a French fabliau; indeed a good one
exists essentially like Chaucer's; though lacking most of his
more vivid points, it might have set his imagination at work.
It is striking that these two successive tales are laid at the
two ancient universities, Oxford and Cambridge.   Chaucer
was learned, extraordinarily well-read, but in spite of his
genuine religious feeling, not interested perhaps in the close
and mostly theological scholarship which flourished there.
The clerk "hende" ("nice") Nicolas, who uses his people's
support to dabble in astrology and music, and the less defined
clerks in the other tale are the same bright and active and
attractive type of college student as appeals today to most
people.

The Cook's Tale

The Host, with all respect for decorum and for the quality,
sometimes stows it away, shares the tastes of the vulgar, and
risks falling out by chaffing with them. So he does with the
Cook. The fellow travels with the Haberdasher and his four
mates, to regale them and support their credit for wealth
and luxury,

> And eek hir wyves wolde it wel assente.

The Cook in the General Prologue has a short but typical
description, is merely skilful in his calling, yet with an individual touch—an ulcer on his shin, which has no connection with his calling; then, with a touch of warm-hearted
appreciation—the ulcer was a pity, for he certainly made the
best creamed chicken ever seen.

From the general aspect of the Cook himself, the Host might have foreseen from him such another story as the *Miller's* and *Reeve's,* and he by no means discourages it as he had with the Miller. The characters are vividly introduced, already more worthless and disreputable than those in the two preceding tales, but there is no hint of what is to happen, except that it is likely to be minor crime such as abounds in late medieval popular literature. No one can say whether some such tale was in Chaucer's mind. There is justification for the surmise that he was trying his hand at invention. While the Middle Ages did not specially admire inventiveness in narrative, there was much of it especially in detail and especially of patchwork, reminiscences from here and there worked into unity. Chaucer's narratives are full of such patchwork and also of invented additions. There is the further suggestive fact that almost all his unfinished narrative poems have no known source or close parallel; here I put the *Anelida,* the *House of Fame,* the tale of the Cook, that concerning Sir Thopas, that of the Squire. It is likely enough that, with the Cook, Chaucer planned invention on the basis of such misdeeds of the underworld as there is abundant record of in documents of late medieval London. Chaucer, among English poets, is assuredly in good company in caring less to invent narratives than to add new dimensions to what was already not unfamiliar.

BIBLIOGRAPHY

The edition of Chaucer and the commentary most used are in F. N. Robinson's *Complete Works of Geoffrey Chaucer* (Boston: Houghton Mifflin Co., 1933), extensive, judicious, and conservative. For guidance to earlier scholarly criticism and statement of fact, I refer especially to his Bibliography, pp. 743-746, as well as to his other editorial matter. For supplementary work, especially published later, under each chapter I mention some of the most useful.—J. S. P. Tatlock.

Dr. Tatlock left notes for the bibliographies for Chapters I, III, and IX. The other sections were prepared in accordance with his suggestions and his plan to keep this bibliography very short. For complete surveys of the yearly work on Chaucer from 1925 on, with good summaries and with brief comment on the important contributions, the reader is referred to Dorothy Everett's chapters on Middle English in *The Year's Work in English Studies,* ed. Frederick S. Boas (Oxford University Press).

CHAPTER ONE

Pendrill, Charles. *London Life in the Fourteenth Century.* New York: Adelphi Co., 1925; Besant, Sir Walter. *Mediaeval London.* 2 vols. London: A. & C. Black, 1906; Tout, Thomas F. *Beginnings of a Modern Capital (Proceedings of the British Academy,* XI, 1923): *Chapters in the Administrative History of Mediaeval England.* 6 vols., Manchester: The University Press, 1920-33; and *The English Civil Service in the Fourteenth Century (Bulletin of the Ryland Library,* III [Manchester, 1916-17], 185-214) ; Willard, James F. and

Morris, William A. (eds.) *The English Government at Work, 1327-1336.* Vol. I. Cambridge, Mass.: Mediaeval Academy of America, 1940; Beard, Charles A. *The Office of Justice of the Peace in England.* New York: Columbia University Press, 1904; Putnam, B. H. *Early Treatises on the Practice of the Justices of the Peace in the Fifteenth and Sixteenth Centuries.* Oxford: Clarendon Press, 1924; Gras, Norman S. B. *The Early English Customs System.* Cambridge, Mass.: Harvard University Press, 1918; Trevelyan, George M. *English Social History.* London: Longmans Green & Co., 1943; Leach, Arthur F. *Schools of Medieval England.* New York: Macmillan Co., 1915; Rickert, Edith. "Chaucer at School," *Modern Philology,* XXIX (1932) pp. 257-274; Plimpton, George A. *The Education of Chaucer Illustrated from the Schoolbooks in Use in His Time.* London: Oxford University Press, 1935; Sarton, George. *Introduction to the History of Science,* Vol. III, Part 2. ["The Time of Geoffrey Chaucer, Ibn Khaldūn, and Hasdai Crescas"] Baltimore: Carnegie Institution of Washington, 1948; *Chaucer's World.* compiled by Edith Rickert, ed., Olson, Clair C., and Crow, Martin M., New York: Columbia University Press, 1948; Lowes, John Livingston. *Geoffrey Chaucer and the Development of his Genius.* chap. ii ["The World of Affairs"] Boston: Houghton Mifflin Co., 1934; Schlauch, Margaret. "Chaucer's Doctrine of Kings and Tyrants," *Speculum,* XX (1945), pp. 133-156; Scott, Florence R. "Chaucer and the Parliament of 1386," *Speculum,* XVIII (1943), pp. 80-86.

CHAPTER TWO

On the French Tradition: Lowes, John Livingston. *op. cit.,* Chap. III; Lewis, C. S. *The Allegory of Love.* Oxford: Clarendon Press, 1936, Chap. III.

On the *Book of the Duchess:* Clemen, Wolfgang. *Der Junge Chaucer.* Bochum-Langendreer: H. Poppinghaus, 1938, pp. 29-71; Lowes, John Livingston. *op. cit.,* pp. 116-128; Lewis, C. S. *op. cit.,* pp. 167-170; Birney, Earle. "The Beginnings of Chaucer's Irony," *Publications of the Modern Language Association,* LIV (1939), pp. 637-655, esp. pp. 643-648; Stearns, Marshall W. "Chaucer Mentions a Book," *Modern Language Notes,* LVII (1942), pp. 28-31.

CHAPTER THREE

Hauvette, Henri. *Boccace.* Paris: A. Colin, 1914; Lowes, John Livingston. *op. cit.,* pp. 165-191; Pratt, Robert A. "Chaucer's Use of the *Teseida,*" *Publications of the Modern Language Association,* LXII (1947), pp. 598-621, esp. 608-613; Patch, Howard R. *On Rereading Chaucer.* Cambridge, Mass.: Harvard University Press, 1939, pp. 56-122; Dempster, Germaine. *Dramatic Irony in Chaucer.* Stanford, California: Stanford University Press, 1932, pp. 10-26; Young, Karl. "Chaucer's *Troilus and Criseyde* as Romance," *Publications of the Modern Language Association,* LIII (1938), pp. 38-63; Lewis, C. S. *op. cit.,* pp. 176-197; Kirby, Thomas A. *Chaucer's "Troilus": A Study in Courtly Love.* Louisiana State University Press, 1940; Tatlock, J. S. P. "The People in Chaucer's *Troilus,*" *Publications of the Modern Language Association,* LVI (1941), pp. 85-104; Mizener, Arthur. "Character and Action in the Case of Criseyde," *Publications of the Modern Language Association,* LIV (1939), pp. 65-81; Shanley, James L. "The *Troilus* and Christian Love," *Journal of English Literary History,* VI (1939), pp. 271-281.

CHAPTER FOUR

Clemen, Wolfgang. *op. cit.,* pp. 226-237; Pratt, Robert A. *op. cit.,* pp. 604-605.

CHAPTER FIVE

Clemen, Wolfgang. *op. cit.,* pp. 72-160; Lowes, John Livingston. *op. cit.,* pp. 128-145; Goffin, R. C. "Quiting by Tidings in the *Hous of Fame,*" *Medium Aevum,* XII (1943), pp. 40-44; Pratt, Robert A. "Chaucer's Claudian," *Speculum,* XXII (1947), pp. 419-429, esp. 423-425; Teager, Florence E. "Chaucer's Eagle and the Rhetorical Colors," *Publications of the Modern Language Association,* XLVII (1932), pp. 410-418; Levy, H. L. "As myn auctour seyth," *Medium Aevum,* XII (1943), pp. 25-39; Smyser, H. M. "Chaucer's Two-mile Pilgrimage," *Modern Language Notes,* LVI (1941), pp. 205-207.

CHAPTER SIX

Clemen, Wolfgang. *op. cit.,* pp. 161-205; Lowes, John Livingston. *op. cit.,* pp. 145-156; Bronson, Bertrand H. *In Appreciation of Chaucer's "Parlement of Foules"* (University of California Publications in English, Vol. III, No. 5, 1935), pp. 193-223; and "The *Parlement of Foules* Revisited," *Journal of English Literary History,* XV (1948), pp. 247-260; Pratt, Robert A. "Chaucer's Use of the *Teseida,*" *Publications of the Modern Language Association,* LXII (1947), pp. 598-621, esp. 605-607.

CHAPTER SEVEN

Lowes. *op. cit., pp.* 157-164; Estrich, Robert M. "Chaucer's Prologue to the *Legend of Good Women* and Machaut's *Jugement dou Roy de Navarre,*" *Studies in Philology,* XXXVI (1939), pp. 20-39;

Lossing, Marian. "The Prologue of the *Legend of Good Women* and the *Lai de Franchise*," *Studies in Philology*, XXXIX (1942), pp. 15-35; Callan, Norman. "Thyn owne book: A Note on Chaucer, Gower, and Ovid," *Review of English Studies*, XXII (1946), pp. 269-281; Young, Karl. "Chaucer's Appeal to the Platonic Deity," *Speculum*, XIX (1944), pp. 1-13; Shannon, G. P. "The Heroic Couplet in the Sixteenth and Early Seventeenth Centuries" (Stanford University Dissertation, 1926; also partly printed as "Grimald's Heroic Couplet," *Publications of the Modern Language Association*, XLV [1930], pp. 532-542); Hill, Mary H. "Rhetorical Balance in Chaucer's Poetry," *Publications of the Modern Language Association*, XLII (1927), pp. 845-861.

CHAPTER EIGHT

On Boethius: Patch, Howard R. *The Tradition of Boethius.* New York: Oxford University Press 1935.

On the *Astrolabe:* Elmquist, K. E. "An Observation on Chaucer's Astrolabe," *Modern Language Notes*, LVI (1941), pp. 530-534; Sarton, George. *op. cit.*, pp. 1421-1422, 1424.

On short poems: Clemen, Wolfgang. *op. cit.*, pp. 206-226; Birney, Earle. *op. cit.*, pp. 639-642; Moore, Arthur K. "Chaucer's Lost Songs," *Journal of English and Germanic Philology*, XLVIII (1949), 196-208.

CHAPTER NINE

Manly, John M. and Rickert, Edith. *The Text of the "Canterbury Tales."* Chicago: University of Chicago Press, 1940; Tatlock, J. S. P. "The *Canterbury Tales* in 1400," *Publications of the Modern Language Association*, L (1935), pp. 100-139; Pratt, Robert A., and Young, Karl. "The Literary Framework of the *Canterbury Tales*," in *Sources and Analogues of Chaucer's "Canterbury Tales."* Bryan, W. F., and Dempster, Germaine, eds. Chicago: University of Chicago Press, 1941, pp. 1-81; Lowes, John Livingston, *op. cit.*, pp. 191-207.

On the *Prologue:* Malone, Kemp. "Style and Structure in the Prologue to the *Canterbury Tales*," *Journal of English Literary History*, XIII (1946), pp. 38-45; Hulbert, James R. "Chaucer's Pilgrims," *Publications of the Modern Language Association*, LXIV (1949), pp. 823-828; Tuve, Rosemond. "Spring in Chaucer and Before Him," *Modern Language Notes*, LII (1937), pp. 9-16; Horrell, Joe. "Chaucer's Symbolic Plowman," *Speculum*, XIV (1939), 82-92; Bowden, Muriel, *A Commentary on the General Prologue to the "Canterbury Tales"* (New York: Macmillan Co., 1948).

On the *Knight's Tale:* Pratt, Robert A. "The *Knight's Tale,*" in *Sources and Analogues,* pp. 82-105; "Chaucer's Use of the *Teseida,*" *Publications of the Modern Language Association,* LXII (1947), pp. 613-620; and "Conjectures Regarding Chaucer's Manuscript of the *Teseida,*" *Studies in Philology,* XLII (1945), pp. 745-763; Frost, William. "An Interpretation of Chaucer's *Knight's Tale,*" *Review of English Studies,* XXV (1949), pp. 289-304; French, W. H. "The Lovers in the *Knight's Tale,*" *Journal of English and Germanic Philology,* XLVIII (1949), pp. 320-328.

On the *Miller's Tale:* Thompson, Stith. "The *Miller's Tale,*" in *Sources and Analogues,* pp. 106-123.

On the *Reeve's Tale:* Hart, Walter Morris. "The *Reeve's Tale,*" in *Sources and Analogues,* pp. 124-147; Tolkien, J. R. R. "Chaucer as a Philologist," *Transactions of the Philological Society,* XL (1934), pp. 1-70, esp. 47-54.

On the *Cook's Tale:* Lyon, Earl D. "The *Cook's Tale,*" in *Sources and Analogues,* pp. 148-54.

THE WRITINGS OF J. S. P. TATLOCK

BOOKS

1907 *The Development and Chronology of Chaucer's Works.* London: Kegan Paul for the Chaucer Society.

1909 *The Harleian MS 7334 and Revision of the "Canterbury Tales."* London: Kegan Paul for the Chaucer Society (1909 for the issue of 1904).

1912 *Troilus and Cressida* ("The Tudor Shakespeare"). New York: Macmillan Co.

The Modern Reader's Chaucer: The Complete Poetical Works of Geoffrey Chaucer, now first put into Modern English (with Percy MacKaye). New York: Macmillan Co.

1914 *The Scene of the "Franklin's Tale" Visited.* London: Kegan Paul for the Chaucer Society.

1916 *Representative English Plays from the Middle Ages to the End of the Nineteenth Century* (with Robert G. Martin). New York: Century Co.

1927 *A Concordance to the Complete Works of Geoffrey Chaucer and to the "Romaunt of the Rose"* (with Arthur G. Kennedy). Washington: Carnegie Institution of Washington.

1950 *The Legendary History of Britain: Geoffrey of Monmouth's "Historia Regum Britanniae" and Early Vernacular Versions.* Berkeley: University of California Press.

The Mind and Art of Chaucer. Syracuse: Syracuse University Press.

ARTICLES

1903 "The Dates of Chaucer's *Troilus and Criseyde* and *Legend of Good Women,*" *Modern Philology,* I, pp. 317-329.

1905 "Chaucer's *dremes: lemes,*" *Modern Language Notes,* XX, p. 126.

1906 "The Duration of the Canterbury Pilgrimage," *Publications of the Modern Language Association,* XXI, pp. 478-485.
"Chaucer and Dante," *Modern Philology,* III, pp. 367-372.
"Chaucer's *Vitremyte,*" *Modern Language Notes,* XXI, p. 62.
"Milton's Sin and Death," *Modern Language Notes,* XXI, pp. 239-240.

1908 "Palamon and Arcite," *Modern Language Notes,* XXIII, p. 128.
"Chaucer," *Americana: A Universal Reference Library,* Issued under the Editorial Supervision of the Scientific American. New York: Munn and Co., Vol. V.

1909 "A British Icarus," *Nation,* LXXXIX, p. 404.

1912 "Syntax," *The New Websterian Dictionary.* New York: Abbreviated in *Webster's Home, School, and Office Dictionary.* New York, pp. 10-12.

1913 "Boccaccio and the Plan of Chaucer's *Canterbury Tales,*" *Anglia,* XXXVII, pp. 69-117.
"Astrology and Magic in Chaucer's *Franklin Tale,*" in *Anniversary Papers by Colleagues and Pupils of George Lyman Kittredge.* Boston: Ginn and Co., pp. 339-350.
"Chaucer's *Retractions,*" *Publications of the Modern Language Association of America,* XXVIII, pp. 521-529.
"The Duration of Chaucer's visits to Italy," *Journal of English and Germanic Philology,* XII, pp. 118-121.

1914 "Another Parallel to the First Canto of the *Inferno,*" *Romanic Review,* V, pp. 90-93.
"The Origin of the Closed Couplet in English," *Nation,* XCVIII, p. 390.
"Notes on Chaucer: Earlier or Minor Poems," *Modern Language Notes,* XXIX, pp. 97-101.
"Notes on Chaucer: The *Canterbury Tales,*" *Modern Language Notes,* XXIX, pp. 140-144.
"Philology and the Occult in Roger Bacon," *Open Court,* XXVIII, pp. 538-545.
"Some Medieval Cases of Blood-Rain," *"Classical Philology,* IX, pp. 442-447.

1915 "The Siege of Troy in Elizabethan Literature, especially Shakespeare and Heywood," *Publications of the Modern Language Association*, XXX, pp. 673-770.

"The Welsh *Troilus and Cressida* and its Relation to the Elizabethan Drama," *Modern Language Review*, X, pp. 265-282.

"Bells Ringing without Hands," *Modern Language Notes*, XXX, p. 160.

"Pygmalion and Peregrine," *Nation*, C, p. 197.

"The Association of American University and College Professors," *Michigan Alumnus*, XXI, pp. 239-240.

1916 "The Chief Problem in Shakespeare," *Sewanee Review*, XXIV, pp. 129-147.

"Chaucer and Wyclif," *Modern Philology*, XIV, pp. 257-268.

"Literature and History," *University of California Chronicle*, XVIII, pp. 3-22.

"*Bretherhed* in Chaucer's *Prolog*," *Modern Language Notes*. XXXI, pp. 139-142.

"Puns in Chaucer," in *Flügel Memorial Volume*, Stanford, California: Stanford University Press.

1917 "The Hermaphrodite Rime," *Modern Language Notes*, XXXII, p. 373.

"The Marriage Service in Chaucer's *Merchant's Tale*," *Modern Language Notes*, XXXII, pp. 373-374.

1918 "May in America 1917, a Poem," *California Chapter of Phi Beta Kappa*, pp. 1-4.

"Why America fights Germany," *War Information Series*, No. 15 (March, 1918), pp. 3-13.

1919 "*Purgatorio* XI 2-3 and *Paradiso* XIV 30," *Romanic Review*, X, pp. 274-276.

"Never less Alone than when Alone,' *Modern Language Notes*, XXXIV, p. 441.

1920 "Dante and Guinizelli in Chaucer's *Troilus*," *Modern Language Notes*, XXXV, p. 443.

1921 "The Epilog of Chaucer's *Troilus*," *Modern Philology*, XVIII, pp. 625-659.

"The Source of the Legend and other Chauceriana," *Studies in Philology*, XVIII, pp. 419-428.

"Chaucer's Elcanor," *Modern Language Notes*, XXXVI, pp. 95-97.

"The Intellectual Interests of Undergraduates," *University of California Chronicle*, XXIII, pp. 364-391.

110

"The Poet in the University," *School and Society*, XIII, pp. 387-388.

1922 "The Work and Plans of the Section on Medieval Latin, of the Modern Language Association of America," *Proceedings of the American Philological Association*, LIII, pp. xxix-xxx.

"Under the Sonne," *Modern Language Notes*, XXXVII, p. 377.

"Ravenna and the Dante Centenary," *Stanford Cardinal*, XXXI, pp. 124-125.

"College Honors and Success in Life," *School and Society*, XV, pp. 647-648.

1923 "Epic Formulas, especialy in Layamon," *Publications of the Modern Language Association*, XXXVIII, pp. 494-529.

"Layamon's Poetic Style and its Relations," *Manly Anniversary Studies in Language and Literature*, Chicago: University of Chicago Press, pp. 3-11.

"Dramatic Irony," *University of California Chroncile*, XXV, pp. 212-222.

"The Chaucer Concordance," *Modern Language Notes*, XXXVIII, pp. 504-506.

"Chaucer's Whelp and Lion," *Modern Language Notes*, XXXVIII, pp. 506-507.

1924 "Levenoth and the Grateful Dead," *Modern Philology*, XXII, pp. 211-214.

"The Study of Medieval Latin in American Universities," *Modern Philology*, XXI, pp. 309-315.

"The General Final Examination in the Major Study," *Bulletin of the American Association of University Professors*, X, pp. 609-635.

"Attacks on Lincoln and his Cabinet," *University of California Chronicle*, XXVI, pp. 441-450.

1926 "The Comprehensive Examination," *Bulletin of the Association of American Colleges*, XII, pp. 211-221.

"America's Mediaeval Academy," *The Commonweal*, III, pp. 653-654.

1927 "General Final Examinations and Tutors," *Educational Recorder*, VIII, pp. 3-16.

1928 "The Modern Reader's *King Horn*," *University of California Chronicle*, XXX, pp. 1-45.

"President Neilson of Smith College," *Nation*, CXXVI, pp. 15-17.

1930 "St. Cecilia's Garlands and their Roman Origin," *Publications of the Modern Language Association*, XLV, pp. 169-179.

"Chaucer and the Legenda Aurea," *Modern Language Notes,* XLV, pp. 296-298.

"Twentieth-Century 'Humanism' in Relation to Graduate Study and Research," *Journal of Proceedings and Address of the Association of American Universities,* XXXII, pp. 150-160.

1931 "Certain Contemporaneous Matters in Geoffrey of Monmouth," *Speculum,* VI, pp. 206-224.

"Irish Costume in Lawman," *Studies in Philology,* XXVIII, pp. 587-593.

"Chaucer's 'Bernard the Monk'," *Modern Language Notes,* XLVI, pp. 21-23.

1932 "Mohammed and his Followers in Dante," *Modern Language Review,* XXVII, pp. 186-195.

1933 "The Middle Ages—Romantic or Rationalistic?" *Speculum,* VIII, pp. 295-304.

"The English Journey of the Laon Canons," *Speculum,* VIII, pp. 454-465.

"Geoffrey and King Arthur in *Normannicus Draco,*" *Modern Philology,* XXXI, pp. 1-18, 113-125.

"The Dragons of Wessex and Wales," *Speculum,* VIII, pp. 223-235.

"Muriel, the Earliest English Poetess," *Publications of the Modern Language Association,* XLVIII, pp. 317-321.

1934 "St. Amphibalus," *Essays and Studies, University of California Publications in English,* IV, pp. 249-257, 268-270.

"Geoffrey of Monmouth and the Date of *Regnum Scotorum,*" *Speculum,* IX, pp. 135-139.

"The Last Cantos of the *Purgatorio,*" *Modern Philology,* XXXII, pp. 113-123.

1935 "The *Canterbury Tales* in 1400," *Publications of the Modern Language Association,* L, pp. 100-139.

"Torquato Tasso and Sidney, *Italica,* XII, pp. 74-80.

"The Date of the *Troilus* and Minor Chauceriana," *Modern Language Notes,* L, pp. 277-296.

"Early English in the Universities," *The English Journal,* XXIV, pp. 555-564.

1936 "Chaucer's *Merchant's Tale,*" *Modern Philology,* XXXIII, pp. 367-381.

"Dante's *Terza Rima,*" *Publications of the Modern Language Association,* LI, pp. 895-903.

"The Origin of Geoffrey of Monmouth's Estrildis," *Specu-*

lum, XI, pp. 121-124.

"The Date of Henry I's Charter to London," *Speculum,* XI, pp. 461-469.

"Has Chaucer's *Wretched Engendering* Been Found?" *Modern Language Notes,* LI, pp. 275-284.

"Prairie Crops," *Rockford College Bulletin,* pp. 3-15.

"The Chronicle Misunderstood," *American Historical Review,* XLI, p. 703.

1937 "Interpreting Literature by History," *Speculum,* XII, pp. 390-395.

1938 "Caradoc of Llancarfan," *Speculum,* XIII, pp. 139-152.

"Geoffrey of Monmouth's Motives for Writing his *Historia,*" *Proceedings of the American Philosophical Society,* LXXIX, pp. 695-703.

"Nostra Maxima Culpa," *Publications of the Modern Language Association,* LIII, pp. 1313-1320.

"Graduate Study and Public Responsibility," *Michigan Alumnus,* XLIV, pp. 316-321.

1939 "The Dates of the Arthurian Saints' Legends," *Speculum,* XIV, pp. 345-365.

1940 "Chaucer's Monk," *Modern Language Notes,* LV, pp. 350-354.

"John Matthews Manly (1865-1940)," [Obituary] *American Philosophical Society Yearbook,* pp. 428-431.

1941 "The People in Chaucer's *Troilus,*" *Publications of the Modern Language Association,* LVI, pp. 85-104.

"The *Franklin's Tale*" (with Germaine Dempster), in *Sources and Analogues of Chaucer's "Canterbury Tales,"* Bryan, W. F. and Dempster, Germaine (eds.), The University of Chicago Press, pp. 377-397.

"Is Chaucer's Monk a Monk?" *Modern Language Notes,* LVI, p. 80.

1943 "Geoffrey of Monmouth's *Vita Merlini,*" *Speculum,* XVIII, pp. 265-287.

"The Lunatic Lover," *Essays and Studies, University of California Publications in English,* XIV, pp. 43-48.

1945 "Greater Irish Saints in Lawman and in England," *Modern Philology,* XLIII, pp. 72-76.

"Karl Young" (with George R. Coffman and George La Piana), *Speculum,* XX, pp. 382-383; reprinted in *A Memoir of Karl Young,* New Haven: private print (Yale University Press, 1946), pp. 11-14.

1946 "Mediaeval Laughter," *Speculum,* XXI, pp. 289-294.

REVIEWS

1906 Gray, Charles. *Lodowick Carleill, Michigan Alumnus,* XII, p. 292.

French, John C. *The Problem of the Two Prologues to Chaucer's "Legend of Good Women," Modern Language Notes,* XXI, pp. 58-62.

1907 Schofield, William H. *English Literature from the Norman Conquest to Chaucer, Modern Language Notes,* XXII, pp. 186-189.

1914 Gayley, Charles M. *Francis Beaumont, Michigan Alumnus,* XX, p. 653.

1915 Gauss, Christian. *The German Emperor as Shown in his Public Utterances, Michigan Alumnus,* XXI, p. 380.

1917 Wells, John Edwin. *A Manual of the Writings in Middle English,* 1050-1400, *American Journal of Philology,* XXXVIII, pp. 441-443.

1920 Wells, John Edwin. *First Supplement to a Manual of the Writings in Middle English, 1050-1400, American Journal of Philology,* XL, p. 324.

Grim, Florence M. *Astronomical Lore in Chaucer, Journal of English and Germanic Philology,* XIX, pp. 129-130.

1921 Bayfield, M. A. *A Study of Shakespeare's Versification, Modern Philology,* XVIII, pp. 504-505.

1923 Thorndike, Lynn. *A History of Magic and Experimental Science during the First Thirteen Centuries of our Era, University of California Chronicle,* XXV, pp. 510-512.

1925 Bruce, Harold. *William Blake in This World, University of California Chronicle,* XXVII, pp. 420-421.

1926 Root, Robert K. *The Book of Troilus and Criseyde by Geoffrey Chaucer, Saturday Review of Literature,* III, p. 362.

1927 Manly, John M. *Some New Light on Chaucer, American Historical Review,* XXXII, p. 913.

1928 Patch, Howard R. *The Goddess Fortuna in Mediaeval Literature, Speculum,* III, p. 406.

Paton, Lucy A. *Les Prophécies de Merlin, Speculum,* III, pp. 416-417.

1929 Barnicle, Mary E. *The Seege or Batayle of Troye, Modern Language Review,* XXIV, pp. 74-75.

1932 Laistner, M. L. W. *Thought and Letters in Western Europe, A. D. 500 to 900,* and Wright, F. A. and Sinclair, T. A. *History of Later Latin Literature from the Middle of the*

Fourth to the End of the Seventeenth Century, University of California Chronicle, XXXIV, pp. 95-99.

1934 Robinson, Fred N. (ed.) *The Complete Works of Geoffrey Chaucer, Speculum*, IX, pp. 459-464.

1936 Wells, John Edwin. *Sixth Supplement to a Manual to the Writings in Middle English, 1050-1400 Speculum*, XI, p. 429.

1937 Russell, J. C. *Dictionary of Writers of Thirteenth Century England, Speculum*, XII, p. 413.

Mersand, Joseph. *Chaucer's Romance Vocabulary, Romanic Review*, XXVIII, p. 274.

1939 Wells, John Edwin. *Seventh Supplement to a Manual of the Writings in Middle English, 1050-1400, Speculum*, XIV, p. 397.

1940 Laistner, M. L. W. (ed.). *Bedae Venerabilis Expositio Actuum Apostolorum et Retractatio, Philosophical Review*, XLIX, p. 596.

1942 Parry, John J. (editor and translator). *Andreas Capellanus, The Art of Courtly Love, Speculum*, XVII, pp. 305-308.

Wells, John Edwin. *Eighth Supplement to a Manual of the Writings in Middle English, 1050-1400, Speculum*, XVII, pp 314-315.